HARVEST

Meridel Le Sueur

Painting of Meridel Le Sueur by Jim Erickson

HARVEST

Collected Stories

by

Meridel Le Sueur

West End Press

1977

The writings in this volume have been previously published as follows:

"What Happens in a Strike." **American Mercury,** *Nov. 1934.*

"Women on the Breadlines." **New Masses,** *Jan. 1932.*

"Harvest." **West End,** *Fall 1977.*

"Fudge." **Fantasy,** *Winter 1933.*

"Autumnal Village." **Drafts,** *Oct.-Nov. 1940.*

"God Made Little Apples." **Prairie Schooner,** *Winter 1942.*

"To Hell with You, Mr. Blue!" **Fantasy,** *1941.*

"We'll Make Your Bed." **New Masses,** *May 7, 1946.*

This project is supported by a grant from the National Endowment for the Arts in Washington, D.C., a federal agency.

West End Press, Box 697, Cambridge, Ma. 02139

Table of Contents

**Dedicated to
Rachel and Kenneth
for haven and love**

Publisher's Note

Like the Persephone of her stories, she returns, full of ripeness and bounty in her seventy-seventh year.

Blacklisted for over thirty years, Meridel Le Sueur has kept her art constant. As her stories of the Thirties and Forties are being rediscovered by many of us, so she continues to produce — new glorious novels, poems and personal narratives.

Feminist author Patricia Hampl says of her, "bedecked with Indian turquoise bracelets and rings, a string of large ominous teeth around her neck, a bright multicolored serape covering the body — this walking heap of archetypal images is not your idea of somebody's grandmother. A grandmother, no; a wise and maybe occasionally avenging ancient goddess, yes."

Tom James of Wichita, Kansas, adds: "a beautiful hulk of a woman, as heavy as the sod she knew as a child and as light and graceful as the winds that blow across that sod."

The daughter of the pioneer midwestern educator Marian Wharton, stepdaughter of the socialist Arthur Le Sueur, she has drawn from such divergent streams as the Industrial Workers of the World; her early companions in the Hollywood movie industry of the Twenties; work of writers of that period such as D.H. Lawrence, Willa Cather, Sherwood Anderson; the radicals of the Writers' Congresses of the Thirties, and the militants of the Communist Party of those and later days.

Her social writings of the Thirties reflect a special concern for the situation of women, of all classes and backgrounds but especially the poor and oppressed. This deep identification continues to this day, and will be most powerfully reflected in novels yet to be published.

The present collection brings together Meridel's early writings, from her first story, "Harvest," written in 1929, to "We'll Make Your Bed," which appeared in one of the last issues of *The New Masses* in 1946. A companion volume, also put out by West End, contains her most important writing from 1947 to 1958, the period of political repression which cost her many a job and restricted her publication to the radical press.

This volume contains two pieces of reportage, "What Happens in a Strike" (1934) and "Women on the Breadlines" (1932); four short stories, "Harvest," "Fudge" (1933), "Autumnal Village" (1940) and "God Made Little Apples" (1942); and two humoristic pieces, "To Hell with You, Mr. Blue!" (1941) and "We'll Make Your Bed" (1946).

The right wing of the literary world has sought to bury reportage by claiming it has no literary value. The work of John Reed, Meridel Le Sueur or James Agee hardly needs any defense. A quick eye, a Chaucerian ear informs Meridel's report on women on the breadlines:

> Ellen's friend gets up and goes to the window. She is unbelievably jaunty. I know she hasn't had work since last January. But she has a flair of life in her that glows like a tiny red flame and some tenacious thing, perhaps only youth, keeps it burning bright. . . . She runs wild as a colt hunting pleasure, hunting sustenance.

Meridel's short stories, which have won a wide and appreciative audience from their first entry into the story magazines of the Thirties through *Salute to Spring* (International Publishers, 1940) to their more recent underground existence, are distinguished by a special perception, human emotions caught in flaming language:

> Why should he have to go out, now the summer is going, and shoot at the bright pheasants? I went as far as the spring with him this morning, and there were little cries of birds in the brush and our feet in the dead leaves, and what has happened to me now that my love is a ghost, that the disaster of the Fall makes my blood fall in bitter cascade?
>
> — "Autumnal Village"

Her humoristic writings, on the other hand, capture the broad voice of America in a great continuity with Whitman and Twain, "writers of the people" as Meridel calls them.

> Then I saw her, dangerous and fiery like a flag on a battleship, coming down the hill with our lunch, tough and wiry, my old woman.
> "Jiggers," Slim said, "there's the battle cry. Too late. . . . Prepare to meet thy God."
>
> — "We'll Make Your Bed"

In reading this material over, I have laughed and cried at the points it crosses with my own life, actions, feelings and experience. Every reader will surely do the same. Meridel becomes part of one's life, she cannot be resisted. She expresses the fruition and pain and victory we live by.

West End Press is fortunate to be associated with her.

— John Crawford

What Happens in a Strike

What happens in a strike happens not to one person alone. It is the same all over America. What happens now does not happen from or for a few people. It is a crisis with meaning and potency for all and prophetic of a future. The elements in crisis are the same, there is a fermentation that is identical. The elements are these: a body of men, women and children, hungry; an organization of feudal employers out to break the back of unionization; and the government Labor Board sent to "negotiate" between this hunger and this greed.

When men are hungry they at first mass silently, coming closely together, and then after that they are likely to do something. They are very docile at first, standing together, and then they are not docile any more.

The elements of the Minneapolis strike are identical with those of all recent strikes. The head of the organization of employers, watering his lawn a hot July the first day of the strike said, "We have already collected over $50,000 to break this strike and continue open shop in this city. We don't care about anything but to break this strike." There followed (as in other strikes) paid advertisements in the local papers drawing the red herring across the trail saying, "Let them beware unless an outraged citizenry here take vigorous measures against them."

The strike daily, *The Organizer*, representing the striking union of General Drivers, Helpers, Petroleum and Inside Workers, said, "Fight like one man till victory. We are not fighting an isolated cause. Ours is the cause of the whole labor movement. Should we be defeated other unions would be chopped down one by one. Fight like one man till victory."

Between these two elements a subtle barrage of words. Conferences. With the Labor Board. With the Employers. With the strikers. Cars speeding with ultimatums, with agreements, disagreements. Words like ghouls to cover an old viciousness. Words about rights, justice, freedom. Heirs to Nineteenth Century liberalism said they would deputize and go down and pick off these strikers who dared ask for bread, and do they think they can control our streets, tell us how to run our business?

From the strikers' headquarters, in the heart of the city, straight across from a swanky club, the pickets go out every hour, covering the city, in a systematized network of pickets which was worked out before the strike began. The newspapers said trucking was normal. In reality, not a truck was running.

From the windows of the office buildings towering above strike headquarters, which was only a flat two-storied garage, liberal doctors, lawyers, peer out. "Nothing will happen," they say to each other, but there is expectation in their eyes. "Nothing can happen. This will all be settled square and above board. Why, this is the Twentieth Century! This is a civilized city! This will all be settled over the table."

Women said it was a shame that they could not get things delivered from the stores. The stores put up elegant little signs saying that owing to the strike they thought it best not to deliver goods. This gave the strikers a horse laugh since in the preceding strike they had broken the heads of hundreds of scabs!

The thermometer registered 90°, 98°, then 102°. Not a truck moved.

On Thursday the mayor and the chief of police and the employers got nervous, because nothing was happening. Picketing was peaceful and effective, the men observing the agreement of the Governor and the Labor Board to carry no clubs while negotiations were in progress. They were also urging the police to convoy no trucks, but the police paid no attention.

Then the police staged a show Thursday afternoon, with the ragged pickets looking on from their squad cars. In front of over a hundred cops, before reporters and camera men, they moved 150 pounds of merchandise in a five-ton truck. This was a decoy, supposedly a hospital truck, and the intention was to get the pickets to attack hospital supplies and make good publicity. Amidst a crowd of bystanders and picketers they loaded this truck with one box and it was convoyed, amidst the clicking of cameras, by thirty automobiles filled with cops, guns sticking out like pin cushions.

The picketers did not fall into this trap. The fake movement was a failure. The Labor Board sent out word, received word. The strikers wanted to arm after this. The president of the union said, "I can't understand a word of any of these elegant negotiations. Speak in terms of bread and butter. I'm through listening to words."

The words continued.

2

Strike headquarters is a dark old garage, that must have been a stable once. A roadway runs through the center of it where the picketers wait the call that comes from the loudspeaker above the door. One side is roped off. This is the hospital, fitted with one plain table, six cots and an operating table. Buckshot wounds take lots of operating.

An old wooden stairway leads upstairs where there is an improvised auditorium where meetings are held. Here also the loudspeaker penetrates incessantly: "Calling car 31. Calling car 31. Calling picket car 20. Wanted a driver and a helper. Wanted a driver and a helper . . . a driver and a helper right away. All right, fellows, we have a driver and a helper. Now let's everybody be quiet. Stand by folks for further announcements. Calling Danny. Calling Danny. His family want him to phone right away. We might as well announce right now that we can't call husbands unless they have been away four nights running. Wives remember that picketing is no grounds for divorce."

The loudspeaker also throws the voice down into the street, into an area of one block, which is packed with people, standing in the hot sun, hour after hour, listening to the strike broadcast, watching the picket cars swing out of the black doorway, packed with hot, wild-looking boys, drunk with fatigue.

Upstairs also there are cots on which lie sleeping boys and men. In the rear is the commissary where at a small counter with two hundred tin cups and less plates over three thousand men are fed daily.

If you think that the commissary is organized like a church supper you are mistaken. Most of these men and women have spent years in industry, and specialization, organization, and efficiency have been ground into their bones.

Women are making sandwiches, two are pouring coffee and buttermilk to the thick line of men, passing rapidly by, filling their cups, getting sandwiches, passing on, to squat down in the hall eating. Two are washing the tin cups as fast as they are brought back and piling them up by the pourers again. The line is heavy. The men pass down, tense, orderly. The silence is continued, the voice of the announcer penetrates. Everyone is still, listening. "Move on down, give the other fellow a chance." They move on and take their grub towards a window.

Somebody shouts, "For Christ's sake, look at that." Somebody has thrown the dregs of their coffee out the open window on to the alley below. A cry goes up. The foreman, an efficient stout woman, bawls out the offender like any mother, and they all listen, as if they were all ashamed. No one else will throw dregs or crumbs out of the window. "You aren't dry behind the ears yet," she says. "Don't you know we have to keep order here?"

The heat is intense, 114°. Nobody says a word about it. An oldish man mumbles while he is trying to get a ham sandwich instead of a cheese: "After yesterday they is sure going to be trouble," he says. "I wish I was out in the country." A young buck says fiercely, throwing sugar in his coffee, "No you don't wish you was in the country. You wish you was right here, where you belong." "Yes, sure," the old man says, "But they is going to be trouble." "Right here is where you belong, with all the fellows," the young man says, pushing him on down the line ahead of him.

There is a sign on the wall saying, "NO DRINKING. YOU'LL NEED ALL YOUR WITS." And there is not a breath, amongst all these hearty bucks, used to roustering perhaps and drinking, there is not a fight and not a breath. There is silence, every man listening to the announcer who now is analyzing the reports, the statements, counterstatements in the morning papers. Some of them stand reading the wall bulletins, and copies of *The Organizer*, the daily strike paper, one of the first daily papers ever edited in a strike.

The paper has the current news on what the Labor Board is doing, editorials, comment. A market has been set up where the farmer brings his produce and sells directly to consumer. Besides, the farmers bring in fresh stuffs and meat and eggs to the strikers. An item tells how the men go out and round up produce.

Nob, Moas and Hanson have been doing a splendid job touring Pine County and collecting food for the Commissary. They say they get a wonderful reception wherever they go. Every farmer is interested in our struggle and anxious to help out. All day long they collect vegetables and at night they gather together with a group of farmers to butcher and dress the livestock brought in from various farms. This work they do by the light of automobile lamps, lubricated occasionally by some wonderful home brew!

Another item:

One of the rats finking for Pratts lived off our Commissary for a week. That's a man for you!

A letter from a farmer to the union:

This isn't much of a donation but all we have, times aren't so good for vegetables on the farm owing to the drouth. But we are 100 percent with you in your struggle. You must win.

We folks in Polk county have put up some brave fights. The paper don't tell you city fellows the truth about us but we assure you we are brothers to you; we will fight together to the end.

Another:

Asbestos Workers Local donates ten dollars to the strike fund.

And this:

Farrell Dobbs was found asleep hanging from a hook in the repair department last night. He says he has lost all use for beds.

And there is a serial letter than is run every day from one of the strikers named Mike to his dere emily. It runs:

Here i am at strike head ¼ an its plenty hot. Hell emily i bin thinkin the last few days. these here bosses we got in town keep yellin in the papers and over there radios that communism and payin 54½c an hour is one an the same thing. well if thats what communism is, why i gess im a Communist an i expec most evry one in the world excep a small bunch of pot-bellyd and titefisted bosses must be to.

enyways we got the town tied up tighter then a bulls eye in fly time. . . .

A woman comes into the Commissary with her young baby to get the bottle warmed. Some young girls are asleep on a cot in the corner. They wear overalls and have been on picket duty. One girl says, "I come down today. My dad's been gone six days, and three days ago my ma left to work in the hospital and so I come today. I'm going to be in on it too.''

Thousands of men pour down the line for lunch. The dishwater becomes black and smelling of buttermilk. It is 115° with the sun beating in. Don't spit on the floor, you lunkhead, what do you think this is? Feelings are quick and fluid, the air intense to carry meaning. Eyes looking, hands raising a thousand cups, throats burning, eyes bloodshot, the body dilated to catch every sound over the whole city. They are expecting something to happen.

Nobody knows he is tired. Nobody knows he is hot. We are all swung into the most intense and natural organization I have ever seen. These men are on the spot, acting on their own, visible and known within the city, acting outwardly and militantly for all, and they know it. I remember hearing once how the Russian peasants walked into the cities after the Revolution, saying this is our responsibility now. This is organization that comes naturally from the event, of thousands of men conducting themselves as one man, disciplining themselves out of innate and peculiar responsibility. What is done by one member is instantly known by all. This is a quickening of the social body, this is an enlivening of the social responsibility.

It is one o'clock. Pickets have been pouring out down to the market now for two hours. Everyone is sure something is about to happen. The men bolt their lunches. You can feel the continual drain of men from the hall. The women go out in front whenever they can to see what is happening. More women, feeling something in the air, come down to be near their men. Waiting at home you get nervous and you can't hear what is going on. Out in the country thousands of farmers are sitting at their radios and will know what is about to happen almost before the extras are on the street.

Pickets continue to pour into the market area. Hundreds of men are poured out of the building and hundreds pour in filling the ranks as fast as they are emptied. The hall is very quiet now. The excited steady voice of the announcer calling cars, calling men. You cannot see men any more, only the forward-going body, the face marked by one emotion. Reports like wildfire spread. The announcer says that hundreds of cops are now in the market area armed with sawed-off shotguns.

At five minutes to two the pickets are still silently pouring out on to the line.

The doctors and lawyers were looking out of their office windows on to the street saying nothing could happen. Six liberals were sitting in a newspaper office saying that we should *vote* a change, ballots and not bullets, they said. And they were drawn from their chairs like dummies on steel wires, by shots that lasted continuously and thickly for five full minutes. Two blocks away at the hotel the negotiators stopped their words. The women shopping on the avenue swerved, moved, listened. For five minutes the cops fired into unarmed pickets and bystanders.

3

What had happened was this: Police and pickets gathered at the market because a truck was about to be moved. The chief of police said, "We're going to start moving goods. You men have guns and you know what to do with them. When we are finished with this there will be other goods to move."

The design moved toward a crisis, clotted in centrifugal movement congealed, twisted together with horrific fury. When this movement was over every person within one hundred miles would be changed, the shape and substance of everything different. Words no longer have any meaning, for the distance is shortening between the word and the catastrophe. With a hunger now for the real happening, men, and strikers, gather at the market. Clots of them standing protective on the street, yet all moving within themselves, the cops moving in an outer circle of known authority, the picketers moving within the mass of townsfolk, a glowing mass, without visible command, yet bound together in a powerful impulse, following a design in their movement which goes from separateness, congealing swiftly into a massed and integrated form.

The police pointing the muzzles of shotguns tried to hold the circling crowd back and the pickets away. It was 102° in the shade. The sidewalk bubbled. An area was made in the center of the street by the police for this visible action which was about to show a real temper and a known intention. In that area it was about to happen.

A squad car of pickets waited in an alley for that truck to move. The truck drew up at the warehouse, was loaded, began slowly to move surrounded by police, by pointed shotguns. The picket truck moved forward to stop it, jammed into the truck and the picketers swarmed off; but instantly stopping them in mid-movement, the cops opened fire, splaying them with buckshot. The movement stopped, severed, dismayed. Two boys fell back into their own truck. The swarm broke, cut into, whirled up, eddied, fell down soundlessly. The eyes closed as in sleep, and when they opened, men were lying crying in the street with blood spurting from the myriad wounds buckshot makes. Turning instinctively for cover they were shot in the back. And into that continued fire flowed the next line of pickets to pick up their wounded. They flowed directly into that buckshot fire, inevitably, without hesitation as one wave follows another. And the cops let them have it as they picked up their wounded. Lines of living, solid men fell, broke, wavering, flinging up, breaking over with the curious and awful abandon of despairing gestures, a man stepping in the street, another holding his severed arm in his other hand.

Another line came in like a great wave and the police kept firing. As fast as they broke that strong cordon it gathered again. Wherever it was smashed the body filled again, the tide fell and filled. Impelled by that strong and terrific union they filled in every gap like cells in one body healing itself. And the cops shot into it again and again. Standing on the sidewalk, no one could believe that he was seeing this. Until he himself was hit. Three blocks away business was moving thickly, women were shopping.

In ten minutes the militia appeared over the bridge, swarmed out of their trucks, with order to "deploy as skirmishers." They stretched across the streets and sidewalks. They carried bomb guns, automatics, rifles with set bayonets, sub-machine guns and mounted on the trucks were machine guns.

The food truck and convoy only then began to move. The strikers stirred. From each police car shotguns were trained on the pickets. The truck rushed by.

The wounded were arrested for being shot. They were searched. Not a picket was armed with so much as a toothpick.

They had believed the words.

4

At headquarters the wounded were brought in. "This is murder," the announcer shouted. Men were lying on the floor. Forty-eight unarmed workers had been wounded. There were only two doctors and two nurses.

The next day the words started again. Words that were now proven to be crawling with maggots, so rotten in the warp and woof murderers could come and go without detection. The Mayor said the police did not carry guns for ornament. The Governor gently rebuked the city, saying there had been a truce. The Labor Board said there had been a truce. The Labor Board said there had been a truce. The Employers' Committee said they had never heard of a truce. The chief of police said it was his duty to protect life and property.

The strikers said, "Did you hear the story?" "No, what?" "A woman married a cop!"

The skirts of the women had blood on them. The floor of the strike headquarters had blood on it. Already myth was growing up around the afternoon. Black Friday the men called it. The boys got out their billies which had been taken away from policemen in a previous strike. Some began to make designs of how to make a kind of dagger with an ice pick and a bit of leather. A line formed outside the hospital to give blood transfusions to the wounded.

On Saturday Henry Ness, father of four children, war veteran, died with thirty-eight slugs in his body. The temper of headquarters changed. In black letters *The Organizer* said, WORKERS' BLOOD IS SHED. THE FIGHT HAS JUST BEGUN. THE FIRST MARTYR. Four times as many pickets massed as there had been before. Night and day workers carrying their children held them up to see the body of Henry Ness.

The following Tuesday, labor followed the funeral cortege that took three hours in passing. Six solid blocks of overalled men, a solid block of women and children four abreast. Thousands of women looked out of their windows at the cortege. Thousands of men stood on the sidewalks. Children stopped skipping rope, a ball in hand, and watched, and there was not a sound. There was a silence slowly being filled with the awful condemnation of thousands of people.

A grim silence stood in the afternoon that frightened the city. Thousands marching in meticulous order, in a strange pattern, without coercion, the drama forming from deep instinctive and unified forces of real and terrible passion.

Silently, with the delicate muffled sound of many feet, past the stop and go signs that clicked mechanically, went

the marching crowd. Not a policeman was in sight. Some
said the chief was out of town. They trafficked their own
cortege with miraculous, with spontaneous order. Where
there was a gap a man sprang into it. No one had a name
except the name of sorrow and the name of action.

They marched straight through the heart of the city
holding up Loop traffic for over three hours. Streetcars
lined the city for blocks. Conductors got out of their cars
and trafficked the street nearest them.

A man with a number of badges tried to break
through the line at one time where the cortege had stopped
for a moment and instantly his car was covered like a
rotten thing in fly time and men with baseball bats ordered
him back saying that no man was going to break the cortege of labor. A man did not dare put on his hat until the
whole cortege had passed, or he was in danger of having it
knocked off for him.

Some told and retold the story of the shooting to each
other, the women marching, men and women on the
sidewalk. They said over and over, repeated, echoed,
carried down the long line of march. "We won't *never*
forget this. We won't never forget this . . ."

When men are hungry, one man dead in their cause
will make living and dangerous men of slaves or skeletons.

Women on the Breadlines

I am sitting in the city free employment bureau. It's the women's section. We have been sitting here now for four hours. We sit here every day, waiting for a job. There are no jobs. Most of us have had no breakfast. Some have had scant rations for over a year. Hunger makes a human being lapse into a state of lethargy, especially city hunger. Is there any place else in the world where a human being is supposed to go hungry amidst plenty without an outcry, without protest, where only the boldest steal or kill for bread, and the timid crawl the streets, hunger like the beak of a terrible bird at the vitals?

We sit looking at the floor. No one dares think of the coming winter. There are only a few more days of summer. Everyone is anxious to get work to lay up something for that long siege of bitter cold. But there is no work. Sitting in the room we all know it. That is why we don't talk much. We look at the floor dreading to see that knowledge in each other's eyes. There is a kind of humiliation in it. We look away from each other. We look at the floor. It's too terrible to see this animal terror in each other's eyes.

So we sit hour after hour, day after day, waiting for a job to come in. There are many women for a single job. A thin sharp woman sits inside a wire cage looking at a book. For four hours we have watched her looking at that book. She has a hard little eye. In the small bare room there are half a dozen women sitting on the benches waiting. Many come and go. Our faces are all familiar to each other, for we wait here every day.

This is a domestic employment bureau. Most of the women who come here are middle aged, some have families, some have raised their families and are now alone, some have men who are out of work. Hard times and the man leaves to hung for work. He doesn't find it. He drifts on. The woman probably doesn't hear from him for a long time. She expects it. She isn't surprised. She struggles alone to feed the many mouths. Sometimes she gets help from the charities. If she's clever she can get herself a good living from the charities, if she's naturally a lick spittle, naturally a little docile and cunning. If she's proud then she starves silently, leaving her children to find work, coming home after a day's searching to wrestle with her house, her children.

Some such story is written on the faces of all these women. There are young girls too, fresh from the country. Some are made brazen too soon by the city. There is a great exodus of girls from the farms into the city now. Thousands of farms have been vacated completely in Minnesota. The girls are trying to get work. The prettier ones can get jobs in the stores when there are any, or waiting on table, but these jobs are only for the attractive and the adroit. The others, the real peasants, have a more difficult time.

Bernice sits next to me. She is a Polish woman of thirty-five. She has been working in people's kitchens for fifteen years or more. She is large, her great body in mounds, her face brightly scrubbed. She has a peasant mind and finds it hard even yet to understand the maze of the city where trickery is worth more than brawn. Her blue eyes are not clever but slow and trusting. She suffers from loneliness and lack of talk. When you speak to her, her face lifts and brightens as if you had spoken through a great darkness, and she talks magically of little things as if the weather were magic, or tells some crazy tale of her adventures on the city streets, embellishing them in bright colors until they hang heavy and thick like embroidery. She loves the city anyhow. It's exciting to her, like a bazaar. She loves to go shopping and get a bargain, hunting out the places where stale bread and cakes can be had for a few cents. She likes walking the streets looking for men to take her to a picture show. Sometimes she goes to five picture shows in one day, or she sits through one the entire day until she knows all the dialog by heart.

She came to the city a young girl from a Wisconsin farm. The first thing that happened to her, a charlatan dentist took out all her good shining teeth and the fifty dollars she had saved working in a canning factory. After that she met men in the park who told her how to look out for herself, corrupting her peasant mind, teaching her to mistrust everyone. Sometimes now she forgets to mistrust everyone and gets taken in. They taught her to get what she could for nothing, to count her change, to go back if she found herself cheated, to demand her rights.

She lives alone in little rooms. She bought seven dollars' worth of second-hand furniture eight years ago.

She rents a room for perhaps three dollars a month in an attic, sometimes in a cold house. Once the house where she stayed was condemned and everyone else moved out and she lived there all winter alone on the top floor. She spent only twenty-five dollars all winter.

She wants to get married but she sees what happens to her married friends, left with children to support, worn out before their time. So she stays single. She is virtuous. She is slightly deaf from hanging out clothes in winter. She had done people's washings and cooking for fifteen years and in that time saved thirty dollars. Now she hasn't worked steady for a year and she has spent the thirty dollars. She had dreamed of having a little house or a houseboat perhaps with a spot of ground for a few chickens. This dream she will never realize.

She has lost all her furniture now along with the dream. A married friend whose husband is gone gives her a bed for which she pays by doing a great deal of work for the woman. She comes here every day now sitting bewildered, her pudgy hands folded in her lap. She is hungry. Her great flesh has begun to hand in folds. She has been living on crackers. Sometimes a box of crackers lasts a week. She has a friend who's a baker and he sometimes steals the stale loaves and brings them to her.

A girl we have seen every day all summer went crazy yesterday at the Y.W. She went into hysterics, stamping her feet and screaming.

She hadn't had work for eight months. "You've got to give me something," she kept saying. The woman in charge flew into a rage that probably came from days and days of suffering on her part, because she is unable to give jobs, having none. She flew into a rage at the girl and there they were facing each other in a rage both helpless, helpless. This woman told me once that she could hardly bear the suffering she saw, hardly hear it, that she couldn't eat sometimes and had nightmares at night.

So they stood there, the two women, in a rage, the girl weeping and the woman shouting at her. In the eight months of unemployment she had gotten ragged, and the woman was shouting that she would not send her out like that. "Why don't you shine your shoes," she kept scolding the girl, and the girl kept sobbing and sobbing because she was starving.

"We can't recommend you like that," the harrassed Y.W.C.A. woman said, knowing she was starving, unable to do anything. And the girls and the women sat docilely, their eyes on the ground, ashamed to look at each other, ashamed of something.

Sitting here waiting for a job, the women have been talking in low voices about the girl Ellen. They talk in low voices with not too much pity for her, unable to see through the mist of their own torment. "What happened to Ellen?" one of them asks. She knows the answer already. We all know it.

A young girl who went around with Ellen tells about seeing her last evening back of a cafe downtown, outside the kitchen door, kicking, showing her legs so that the cook came out and gave her some food and some men gathered in the alley and threw small coin on the ground for a look at her legs. And the girl says enviously that Ellen had a swell breakfast and treated her to one too, that cost two dollars.

A scrub woman whose hips are bent forward from stooping with hands gnarled like watersoaked branches clicks her tongue in disgust. No one saves their money, she says, a little money and these foolish young things buy a hat, a dollar for breakfast, a bright scarf. And they do. If you've ever been without money, or food, something very strange happens when you get a bit of money, a kind of madness. You don't care. You can't remember that you had no money before, that the money will be gone. You can remember nothing but that there is the money for which you have been suffering. Now here it is. A lust takes hold of you. You see food in the windows. In imagination you eat hugely; you taste a thousand meals. You look in windows. Colors are brighter; you buy something to dress up in. An excitement takes hold of you. You know it is suicide but you can't help it. You must have food, dainty, splendid food and a bright hat so once again you feel blithe, rid of that ratty gnawing shame.

"I guess she'll go on the street now," a thin woman says faintly, and no one takes the trouble to comment further. Like every commodity now the body is difficult to sell and the girls say you're lucky if you get fifty cents.

It's very difficult and humiliating to sell one's body.

Perhaps it would make it clear if one were to imagine having to go out on the street to sell, say, one's overcoat. Suppose you have to sell your coat so you can have breakfast and a place to sleep, say, for fifty cents. You decide to sell your only coat. You take it off and put it on your arm. The street, that has before been just a street, now becomes a mart, something entirely different. You must approach someone now and admit you are destitute and are now selling your clothes, your most intimate possessions. Everyone will watch you talking to the stranger showing him your overcoat, what a good coat it is. People will stop and watch curiously. You will be quite naked on the street. It is even harder to try to sell one's self, more humiliating. It is even humiliating to try to sell one's labor. When there is no buyer.

The thin woman opens the wire cage. There's a job for a nursemaid, she says. The old gnarled women, like old horses, know that no one will have them walk the streets with the young so they don't move. Ellen's friend gets up and goes to the window. She is unbelievably jaunty. I know she hasn't had work since last January. But she has a flare of life in her that glows like a tiny red flame and some tenacious thing, perhaps only youth, keeps it burning bright. Her legs are thin but the runs in her old stockings are neatly mended clear down her flat shank. Two bright spots of rouge conceal her pallor. A narrow belt is drawn tightly around her thin waist, her long shoulders stoop and the blades show. She runs wild as a colt hunting pleasure, hunting sustenance.

It's one of the great mysteries of the city where women go when they are out of work and hungry. There are not many women in the bread line. There are no flop houses for women as there are for men, where a bed can be had for a quarter or less. You don't see women lying on the floor at the mission in the free flops. They obviously don't sleep in the jungle or under newspapers in the park. There is no law I suppose against their being in these places but the fact is they rarely are.

Yet there must be as many women out of jobs in cities and suffering extreme poverty as there are men. What happens to them? Where do they go? Try to get into the Y.W. without any money or looking down at heel. Charities take care of very few and only those that are called "deserving." The lone girl is under suspicion by the virgin women who dispense charity.

I've lived in cities for many months broke, without help, too timid to get in bread lines. I've known many women to live like this until they simply faint on the street from privations, without saying a word to anyone. A woman will shut herself up in a room until it is taken away from her, and eat a cracker a day and be as quiet as a mouse so there are no social statistics concerning her.

I don't know why it is, but a woman will do this unless she has dependents, will go for weeks verging on starvation, crawling in some hole, going through the streets ashamed, sitting in libraries, parks, going for days without speaking to a living soul like some exiled beast, keeping the runs mended in her stockings, shut up in terror in her own misery, until she becomes too super-sensitive and timid to even ask for a job.

Bernice says even strange men she has met in the park have sometimes, that is in better days, given her a loan to pay her room rent. She has always paid them back.

In the afternoon the young girls, to forget the hunger and the deathly torture and fear of being jobless, try to pick up a man to take them to a ten-cent show. They never go to more expensive ones, but they can always find a man willing to spend a dime to have the company of a girl for the afternoon.

Sometimes a girl facing the night without shelter will approach a man for lodging. A woman always asks a man for help. Rarely another woman. I have known girls to sleep in men's rooms for the night on a pallet without molestation and be given breakfast in the morning.

It's no wonder these young girls refuse to marry, refuse to rear children. They are like certain savage tribes, who, when they have been conquered, refuse to breed.

Not one of them but looks forward to starvation for the coming winter. We are in a jungle and know it. We are beaten, entrapped. There is no way out. Even if there were a job, even if that thin acrid woman came and gave everyone in the room a job for a few days, a few hours, at thirty cents an hour, this would all be repeated tomorrow, the next day and the next.

Not one of these women but knows that despite years of labor there is only starvation, humiliation in front of them.

Mrs. Grey, sitting across from me, is a living spokesman for the futility of labor. She is a warning. Her hands are scarred with labor. Her body is a great puckered scar. She has given birth to six children, buried three, supported them all alive and dead, bearing them, burying them, feeding them. Bred in hunger they have been spare, susceptible to disease. For seven years she tried to save her boy's arm from amputation, diseased from tuberculosis of the bone. It is almost too suffocating to think of that long close horror of years of child-bearing, child-feeding, rearing, with the bare suffering of providing a meal and shelter.

Now she is fifty. Her children, economically insecure, are drifters. She never hears of them. She doesn't know if they are alive. She doesn't know if she is alive. Such subtleties of suffering are not for her. For her the brutality of hunger and cold. Not until these are done away with can those subtle feelings that make a human being be indulged.

She is lucky to have five dollars ahead of her. That is her security. She has a tumor that she will die of. She is thin as a worn dime with her tumor sticking out of her side. She is brittle and bitter. Her face is not the face of a human being. She has borne more than it is possible for a human being to bear. She is reduced to the least possible denominator of human feelings.

It is terrible to see her little bloodshot eyes like a beaten hound's, fearful in terror.

We cannot meet her eyes. When she looks at any of us we look away. She is like a woman drowning and we turn away. We must ignore those eyes that are surely the eyes of a person drowning, doomed. She doesn't cry out. She goes down decently. And we all look away.

The young ones know though. I don't want to marry. I don't want any children. So they all say. No children. No marriage. They arm themselves alone, keep up alone. The man is helpless now. He cannot provide. If he propagates he cannot take care of his young. The means are not in his hands. So they live alone. Get what fun they can. The life risk is too horrible now. Defeat is too clearly written on it.

So we sit in this room like cattle, waiting for a non-existent job, willing to work to the farthest atom of energy, unable to work, unable to get food and lodging, unable to bear children — here we must sit in this shame looking at the floor, worse than beasts at a slaughter.

It is appalling to think that these women sitting so listless in the room may work as hard as it is possible for a human being to work, may labor night and day, like Mrs. Gray wash streetcars from midnight to dawn and offices in the early evening, scrub for fourteen and fifteen hours a day, sleep only five hours or so, do this their whole lives,

and never earn one day of security, having always before
them the pit of the future. The endless labor, the bending
back, the water-soaked hands, earning never more than a
week's wages, never having in their hands more life than
that.

It's not the suffering of birth, death, love that the
young reject, but the suffering of endless labor without
dream, eating the spare bread in bitterness, being a slave
without the security of a slave.

Harvest

It was almost noon and the sun stood hot above the fields. The men would be coming in from the corn for dinner.

Ruth Winji stooped at the bean vines thinking she had not enough yet in her basket for a mess of beans. From the hour's picking of berries and beans she had leaned over in her own heat and the sun's heat driving through her until earth memory and seed memory were in her in the hot air and she was aware of all that stood in the heat around her, the trees in the bright sun, earth-rooted, swaying in sensitive darkness, the wheat like a sea in the slight wind, the cows peering from the caverns of shade of the grove behind the barns with their magic faces and curved horns. Root darkness. Tree darkness. Sun. Earth. Body. She thought: *And my body dark in the sun, root-alive, opening in the sun dark at its deep roots*, and it pained her now that she had quarrelled with her husband.

Anxiously she lifted her large fair torso looking for her young husband as he would come from the corn and wheat, swaying a little as he walked, the sun flashing up the stalk of his body, trying not to show the joy he had walking toward her. By noon she always looked to see him come back, for they had not been separated longer in the six months of their marriage. She shaded her face to see him but she could not tell him at that distance from the other two men that worked in the corn. Still she looked trying to find out what he would be doing for she grieved that a quarrel stood up between them, and now she could not tell him that they would have a child.

It was a quarrel about whether he should buy a threshing machine to harvest the ripening wheat. It wasn't that the money was her dowry money; she dreaded the machine. She knew how men came in from riding that monster all day. She had been hired out before her marriage in the three years since she had come from Bohemia and she knew the cold mindless look of them, not in a column of mounting heat as her husband came now to her, a flame from the earth, broken off as if the quick of it had taken to his very flesh.

Her heart went into a great dismay to think of him riding that machine, and she saw with what a glitter that desire sat upon him and her heart was sick. He had never had a machine and now he wanted one, and it was an encroachment like another woman or war.

She leaned over again thrusting her hand in to the warm vine foliage as the berries hung turning away from the heat upon themselves and she plucked them from the short thick stems and they fell sun-heavy in her hand. Her fingers were stained with berry juice and it had run up the naked belly of her arm and dried there.

She could not keep her mind from thinking how more and more now he looked into that catalogue at night where there were pictures shown of all the parts of a thresher. How he looked into this book all the evening without speaking a word.

Their marriage had been wonderful to her in mid-winter. Coming to his farm, snowed in together in January, and it was as if they themselves brought the spring, warming spreading it from their own bodies until it lifted and mounted from the house to the fields, until the whole earth was jutting in green.

Then she had come with him while he plowed and planted or watched him from the windows of the house as if he stood still in union with her as he strode the sun-scarred earth laying it open, the seed falling in the shadows; then at evening he came from them to her, himself half young, half old in the beginnings of his body, his young brows aslant meeting above his nose, his lips full and red, the sun warming and jutting in him too as the spring advanced, and she was not loath to accept him from the fields smelling of salt sweat, and see all that he had planted ripen and grow from that wild heat into the visible· world, bright and green, rising to its flower, and now a child growing unseen but certain.

Still and even now, the knowing and remembering in herself of the way of his walking or the manner of his speech, as if he were out of breath, coming partly from the newness of the language to him and partly from his eagerness to know everything, his terrible cunning to know: That was it, that was what she really feared, his new world cunning to know, that's what made the fear go up her body so she had to lift her heavy shoulders and breathe slowly looking out over the slow sheen of the turning wheat where everything seemed almost dark in the sun. Still she could not see him, only the three tiny figures of the hoeing men far afield in the corn.

Now she felt she was losing him, as if he were falling out of some soft burr, their ancient closed fertile life, being shaken from the old world tree, in ways beyond her, that she would not go.

The days in the early spring had been like great hot needles sewing them close together, in and out, binding them close, piercing through both to the marrow and binding them with the bright day and the dark night. So the earth lay and herself too, marked by the plow. The sun rose molten with intent. The sun went down and the dusk blew scented and low upon them. The light of day spun them together in utter tranquility — until he had to come saying, "What about this machine? They say that the work will be done so quick, you wouldn't believe it. They say it, Ruth. What about it? We have just enough to have it. What about it?"

And it was just as if he were about to betray her and she could say nothing, seeing that look of greed and cunning, and it was no good to argue this or that because everyone threshed his wheat with the big harvester and he would get her to peek into the catalogue and tell her how the thing mowed the wheat in terrible broad swaths and he showed her the picture of the seat where he would sit swaying sensitive in his own rich body from that iron seat and then she wouldn't look. She would turn away in fear and it came to lie heavier in her than her own planting that she bore now to the fourth month.

And he kept saying, "We could get one of those, Ruth. We could save money. We could just get one of those." With his curious way of repeating himself, beginning and ending on the same phrase. "I was over there looking at that machine in town. Pretty good, too. Yah, pretty good. I was over there looking and it was good." At those times she wouldn't know him at all, that sensual light would be gone from his young keen face, the little flicker that came up from his body gone, and he would be smiling, distracted, rubbing his palms together, as if he were falling away from her, out of the column of himself to be lost to her touch.

The salesman had even come and Winji had looked askance, speaking low so the man left quickly and she took it as a good sign.

She saw the sun topping the roof of the barn so she hurried up the lane with her berries and her beans. Then she heard a sound that made her step in fright. She saw

that monster coming slowly up the road making a corru-
gated track. It came as if with no motion of its parts
through the heat. Ruth Winji ran into the cooled house,
closed the door then stood hearing that beat that was like a
heart and yet monstrous. It seemed to be going straight
over the house and she didn't look out until it had passed
and then she saw the monstrous tracks on the road bed.

She remembered her husband had said they were
demonstrating one at Olson's and had wanted her to go
with him to see and she had said she would not go.

She put the beans on and sat down to wait at the
window where she could first see him come up through the
orchard. The sunlight made an under-darkness over the
lower world so it was dark as a plum, the trees still black-
tipped, a sensitive shimmer of darkness like a convulsion
seemed to go over the sun or world beneath the gloom of
sun so Ruth went into a swoon of heat between the bright
upper sun and the painfully sensitive lower darkness.

She must have dozed because she started aware when
her husband stood in the room behind her. She didn't turn
from the window but knew him there in the soft heated
gloom. He hadn't spoken behind her in the room and her
body started alive to him like a blind antenna upreaching.
He touched her shoulder coming from behind her and she
saw his hands burned rosy. She thrust back against him
and he still stood invisible touching her.

There was a drowsiness of noon all about them, the
soft throaty cluck of the hens, the padding of the dog
across the bare swept ground, the crisp whirr of a bird
startled up from noon drowse winging from shadow to
shadow.

She looked up, saw his face, young, dark, mounted
with blood rosy beneath the burned skin, his brows winged
strangely at an angle as she looked up, his full young
mouth curved willfully, his eyes glinting above her like the
eyes of a hawk looking at her from his narrow spare face
coming down on her from above, setting his lips on hers.

"The beans," she cried.

"Never mind," he said enamored, "I turned the fire
off. Never mind."

Her springing up as she had lifted his whole height to
her instantly like a shaft of shadow against the bright
outdoors light. Seeing the straight willful neck, plunging
to the close-cropped round head, springing against his hard
spare sweating body, she pinned him with her arms where
the shirt was set and stuck to his strong back and felt the

winging of the ribs' spare flight, spanning from her hands the hard thin breast.

At table Winji talked with the hired help about the thresher that had gone by. Ruth listened with lowered head.

"My wife here," Winji said, "doesn't want me to buy it. She wants to keep the old way, God knows why."

The other two men looked at her, the full confused woman sitting at table with them. They seemed to hardly dare lay eyes upon her.

"Well, it's a good one for getting work done," said one.

And they went on talking about threshers and their good and bad points and their makes like man enamoured until she said, "Don't talk about it please, don't speak."

"But we will," her husband said leaning towards her, his fork upraised. "And you're going down with me after this meal and see how it goes."

She did not dispute with him before the men.

After the dishes were cleared he said in the kitchen, "Listen Ruth. The thresher is just down the bend. That's the one I've been talking about. Listen Ruth. I wish you would go down there with me."

"No," she said, wiping off the dishpan carefully.

"You go down and look at it with me. I think it's the best thing we should do. Get it. Buy it. You go down, just for my sake."

"No," she said. "No, I don't want to see it. I'm afraid."

He laughed sharply, his white teeth frightening in his red mouth. "Oh, you'll think it's wonderful when you get over that. Why, it's wonderful."

"No," she said. "It's not wonderful to me."

"Think of it," he said, his eyes glistening in that way she had seen, beyond desire for her. "It will bind the sheaves after it has cut the wheat. . . ."

"What," she said, "bind the sheaves. . . ."

"Yes," he nodded and she saw that lust for knowing and what she took for cunning. "Bind the sheaves at the same time."

"At the same time," she repeated stupidly, "without going around again."

"Yes," he almost shouted, "without going around again."

"Think, how many men did it take on your father's place in the old country to harvest the wheat . . ."

"Yes. . . . Yes, I know," she said, wringing her hands. "I used to carry a brown jug to the men full of spring water with a little meal sprinkled in it. . . ."

"You just sit on the machine and pull levers, see. Like this." He sat down and pulled levers with nothing in his hands.

"How do you know how?" she said. "You've been practicing," she cried.

"What of it," he said like a boy, as if he had got hold of something. "What if I have. Come with me, Ruth. It's your money in a way . . ."

"No, no," she said. "It's your money. Do with it as you like. It's yours. You're the master of the house, but don't make me see it. I don't want to see it. I wash my hands. I wash my hands . . ."

He stood grinning, shaking his head, chagrined a little: "But you can't wash your hands of the whole new world . . ."

But nevertheless she cried after him from the kitchen, "No. No, I wash my hands," and he went out slowly from her, bewildered.

In an hour she went with him, prevailed upon by his physical power over her. He took her hand in the road and pulled her along. Her face was partly covered by her blue sun bonnet and she hid the free hand under her apron. When they got there a clot of men gathered over the machine like black bees and she stood back. Winji joined them, hardly concealing his delight, going time and again round and round the machine. It was brand new and glinted monstrously in the light.

"Look Ruth, look," he kept saying to her, running back and pointing things out and then running back to the machine. "Look at this," he would say but she couldn't hear. She watched his face in envy and malice. The other men were laughing at her but she didn't care.

"No, no," she kept saying, half-obscured in her sun bonnet, pulling away as her husband tried to urge her to look closer at the thresher. The other men looked at her full woman's body, awed a little and thinking how the two were so newly married. They stood away from her a little sheep-faced and she stood away from them and the machine.

"Come and touch it," Winji urged.

"No, no," she cried, "I don't want to."

"Why, it won't hurt you," the men said. "Don't be afraid."

She could see her husband was a bit ashamed of her, and chagrined. "You know," he said to the men, apologizing for her, "in the old country we don't have them like this, in the old country . . ."

She saw the men patting him on the back as if he had already bought the thresher, envy showing in their eyes and he grew big from their envy, strutting around the machine, rubbing his palms together, forgetting her for a moment so she went cold with dread, then running to her to propitiate her.

"Come and touch it, isn't it splendid, look at that." She saw the big knives thrusting back movement even in their stillness, and then on driving power and the tiny man-seat hidden inside, where the little living man was supposed to sit and pull the levers as her husband had been showing her. She was revolted.

But he came close to her and she was bewitched still of his body so she let herself be led straight to the giant and saw all its shining steel close to her and her husband took her hand, still stained by berries, and put it on the steel rump and it was hot as fire to the touch so she drew back nursing her hand. The men laughed and her eyes dilated holding to her husband's face but drawing away.

The men were uneasy. "Never mind, Winji," they said, "lots of our women folks takes it that way at first. My wife says her house was buried in dust the first year the thresher come." They laughed uneasily, shifting, and looking from under their brows at the woman. They turned with ease back to the machine.

She started away down the road. At the bend she turned and looked back and to her horror she saw her husband caressing the great steel body. He was dancing, a little quick dance full of desire, and with his quick living hands he was caressing the bright steel where the sun struck and flew off shining from the steel rumps into her eyes like steel splinters so she turned back sickened, but not before she saw him wave to her, a shy lifting of the hand.

She hadn't told him she was going to have a child. She thought of the child now as a weapon.

She waited while the tension went tighter between them subtly, unspoken now, with his saying now and then at breakfast, at dinner, "Have you changed? What have you against it? Is it a beast?"

She wouldn't answer, only turned against him. And then he turned against her, chagrined and lost without her, trying to win her back to his way and she wouldn't come.

She would cajole him, sitting on his lap in the evening when it was too hot to sleep. "Don't do it. Don't get it." But he knew she was playing a trick to get him. Once he got up, setting her on her own feet and walking away, and that night he didn't come in until late and didn't speak to her but went soundly to sleep.

He grew subtle against her, his summer face hot and congealed, his straight burned neck a pillar of blood against her, his brooding body hot from labor, a wall to her now that made her blind and angered.

When he came in from the cattle with the beast smell about him and milk on his shoes and the lustre of living things, she tried to pull him to her again.

At last there was enmity between them. He didn't talk any more about the machine. They sat together at table without speaking and went to bed silently in the late dusk and she thought he would never come to her again. She felt he was betraying all that and her grief was bitter against a new way, terrible in her so she didn't tell him about the child.

Then one day she went to town and came back early to be near him and go on with the fight, to bring it to come, and there she saw the salesman and Winji at the table leaning over the catalogue and figures and before they shut the book she could see the knives and parts of the machine in color. The two men looked at her guiltily. Winji got up and walked with his back to her and stood stock still at the window. The salesman left as quickly as possible and the two of them stood in the room.

"So!" she said bitterly. "You are going to get it."

"Yes!" he said and she could see the blood flush up his bared neck. "Yes, I am."

"So you don't care," she said, shaking bitterly, clenching her hands together, for she could have torn him to pieces standing there presenting his back to her. "You don't care," she said.

"I don't know what that means." Still he didn't face her. He seemed a stranger with his back turned. "It's for our good to get the machine. This is just woman's stubbornness. It will get us on. We will be powerful people in this neighborhood. . . ."

"Powerful . . ." she repeated.

"Yes," he said now, turning to her uneasily but against her.

She began to cry, not lifting her hands.

The sight of her exasperated him. "What are you crying for," he said in real anger but his face looked guilty. "What are you crying for," he shouted, raising his hand. "Stop that bellowing," he swore and struck her.

She recoiled, her face lifted wide to his. He saw her falling back, her great eyes open upon him in grief. He gave a cry and caught her falling arms, thrust her toward himself. Against her he stood straight and she began to cry from her body shaking, rent by the grief in her. He held her and for a moment seemed to know what she had been feeling but it was only for a moment.

Then it was she told him about the child.

He seemed to forget about the machine those long summer days and everything was as it had been before. She looked at him every day and it seemed that it was over. He was bound to her again and she was content.

The wheat hung heavy on the stalk.

She thought he had arranged to have the old red reaper of Olson's and hire many men and she had already spoken for two of the girls to come in and help feed since she was slower on her feet now too.

One day he came in in the early afternoon and she saw he was excited.

He prowled around the house all afternoon and she was uneasy. "Is anything the matter?" she asked him. "No," he said. But when she wasn't looking she caught him looking at her. At supper he said nervously, as if he had been preparing for it the whole afternoon:

"Tomorrow we begin." He kept looking at his coffee but he kept smiling and looking cunningly at her when she wasn't looking.

"Tomorrow?"

"Huh," he grunted.

She set down her knife and fork, unable to eat. "Well?" she said, a cold fear making her hollow.

"I've got a surprise for you," he said.

"A surprise," she said.

"Don't repeat what I say!" he suddenly shouted, threw down his spoon and left the table.

The next morning she woke sitting bolt upright and saw his place beside her empty. She ran to the window but

it was just dawn and she could see nothing. She dressed
and put on the coffee. Still he did not come. Suddenly she
put on a sweater and went as fast as she could down the
lane to the beanfield where she could see the wheat and
there in the field she saw it standing new and terrible,
gleaming amidst the sea of ripe wheat that crested and
foamed gently to its steel prow and receded away in heavy
fruition.

It was over. There it was. She couldn't say why she
was so afraid but she knew it was against her and against
him. It was a new way.

A bevy of men stood around. Then they saw her and
Winji left them and came towards her beckoning, but she
did not move towards him. He came to her.

"Don't be angry, Ruth," he said gently. "We've got
to do it." We can't be behind the times, can we? Now
with the child."

"No," she said. They both knew that the clot of men
around the machine were half-looking their way, waiting
to see what would happen.

"Isn't she a beauty," he said in his broken tongue.

"A beauty," she said.

"For God's sake, do you have to repeat after me for
God's sake," he said, then beseeching, he begged of her
for the first time. "You say it's all right, darling. Ruth,
you say it's all right. We've got to get ahead, you know
that. Now more than ever, haven't we?" he said softly,
standing only a foot away, but she felt his spell.

"Yes, yes," she said in grief, "yes. . . ."

"Go on," she said. "Go on with it."

"But you come down to the fence and see me go down
the field the first time," he begged.

She hated him but she went behind him, seeing his
heels flicker up as he went in haste, eager to be with his new
"beauty."

The mare in the pasture came up and walked near him
and stood sadly with them at the fence whinnying softly as
her master went down the field, letting the air tremble
through her soft nostrils.

Walking away he heard the soft bleat of the mare, felt
the men waiting from the machine and for a moment a
kind of fear struck him through the marrow as he saw the
glistening thing standing to his hand. Down his soft loins,
his vulnerable breast, went a doom of fear and yet an awful
pride, but he felt shaking at the bones, for leaving the

moistness of sleep, the old world of close dreaming in the thick blossomed surface, and the space of mystery where the seed unfolds to the touch in the cool and thick and heavy sap, the world of close dreaming that is like a woman's hair or the breasts of men.

She saw him turn in the sun — wave to her and mount the machine.

Fudge

I heard the story bit by bit, piecing it together and watching Nina Shelley as she moved to her windows, spying back upon the Town that had set her like a fly in amber, hardening in her own and their hatred.

I saw her too when she came to church and how there was a hush and a withdrawing from her, for she was a visible sign of their own lust and had now come into the Town's dreams, with her urgency that had lasted so short a time. They congealed and flowed around her in their bitterness, she, being sign and symbol, set up for all to see on church day and on market day, coming gruesomely for food for spirit and for body, to feed the corpse they had already buried for her. The women never embraced or touched her, and held her off from their children, from their own warm hearths, glad that she, by her sparsity, made their own bitterness seem abundant and rich.

She was always phoning, asking young girls or young school teachers to come over and see her. Not many would go. Some went out of curiosity and perhaps out of sympathy. Then they told what had been said and what had happened. They always made fudge for one thing and sometimes sang hymns and looked at the pictures of Nina Shelley's dead mother and father and cousins and aunts and uncles who never came to see her now but sent her a little money at Christmas. She still did the same things she had been doing when *it* had happened, the things young girls and school teachers used to do.

So I wasn't surprised when she phoned me. Standing on tip-toe in the hall where I could look right across the street and see her house, I heard her voice and felt in it all that had happened to her uncoil and spring out of the darkness, as if it rang still in the body of that disaster.

"Hello, yes, Miss Shelley," I was a young girl then and took upon myself all that had happened to her as a possible thing that might happen to me when things began to happen, and as a thing that would be better than nothing happening at all.

"Hello, hello, talk louder, dearie," said the voice. "This is Miss Shelley. I'm making some candy this afternoon, and I saw you kind of lonesome-like in the yard and thought, well, I'll call her up and ask her to come over this afternoon and we'll make some candy. All right, dearie, all right.''

I could look right across the street and see her house that looked as if it did not enfold or enshrine, but carried a burden it could not name, written on all the low wooden gables, the glassy windows like a sneer and a grimace. Every time I looked I had to taste that evil, bitterly, like some old thing rotting in the house, giving out a smell until everything became musty of it, letting out more of a being in decay than its wholeness ever had.

There were many in the Town who thought they knew about that moment when something had happened and then stopped happening to Miss Shelley, so she had to spit upon all that was in the Town and look askance at what was growing, putting upon it an evil and a disillusionment. People carried cunning pieces of that design of what had happened; and the worst of it was, she never knew who carried which piece. And she herself became lost in the confusion of what had happened and the myth and dream that had grown in herself mixed with the things people made up about it. So after a time it seemed that every person had a part of the design distorted and shaped to his or her own image.

What had happened I imagine had been more than the Town could imagine and less than they rolled so glibly on their tongues. I felt myself, looking at it from the point of being a young girl, a little younger than Miss Shelley herself had been when it had happened to her, that possibly she had only tried once to step out of herself and that time had curdled and embittered her. So she peered out now with malice, seeing the doings of the Town, knowing them all to be on the way to death and believing not one thing was let off from that curse. Malice then would be the cover of pity in her for what she knew to be in the world, and unwittingly she would pass on to the young girls who came to her the thing that had defiled her, having nothing in her hands but that defilement.

With intricate care, feeling it was a thing could happen to any young girl, I put the pieces together one person saying one thing, another adding to the pattern a bitter bit, another taking that away.

When Miss Shelley had been a girl with puffed sleeves, and an eye out like any other for what could be for her, she hadn't wanted more than to touch, to be made to move like wind and fire with grace toward what might be rich.

I thought that when she had been a young girl that she might have stood in front of her mirror as I stood, letting down her hair, waiting for that fulfillment, as I waited too, and all the time walking amidst the malice that stood ready to ensnare her, and the defeat that was bred more deeply than she knew. Perhaps she had been full of terror, as I was too, seeing that what stood up in her dreams had no reality in the lives of the Town, and imagining, as I imagined too, that there might be some sin that would make her life fettered and barren; yet examining what was in her she must have found, as I did, that there was only goodness in her ways.

Then it must have come upon her swift as a fire I once saw consume a child, leaping to the skirts and quicker than movement, lick, grow upon what it fed, until the hair stood on end, aflame. From the moment that summer when she had first seen Watson Hawk, standing on the church steps, his wild face had fled down her blood, to be there all her life. When he would not have known her on the street, or standing up amongst old ladies in a parlor, his face would be plunging through her, a knife cutting her down.

I knew how she must have looked his way at the band concerts, amidst the circling summer dresses of girls walking arm in arm, swishing on, looking back. And she had to follow him, being drawn, going down the streets of the Town on summer nights looking for his face, asking for that doom until all the men in front of the livery stable were laughing, winking as she passed, slapping their thighs, seeing that strained girl's face looking for Hawk, asking it of him, watching and glad to see her come upon this snare, seeing that she would be entrapped as they had been, and would be one of them.

The Town had wrapped itself warmly in what had happened after that. There were many tales. What had it been? The tongues clacked, striking flint on flint. After Hawk shot her or she shot herself, the carriages had driven slowly past the Shelley house, peering at every stick to find it out, to taste what had happened, what had been known. And even to this day I peered at every doorway of that house and at every bone and piece of skin of Nina Shelley as if they would give up that secret at last and it could be spoken for her and for us all.

Like a pack of starved wolves they fed on her then and after until she wore as thin as a bone.

After they brought her back where she had been found lying in that shed beside the railroad, people had gotten shreds of it all in their teeth worrying it to find what each part belonged to and what the meaning could be.

As well as I could find out, it seems that she had followed Hawk after something had or had not happened between them one day when she had gone on a buggy ride with him out to Mumser's Orchard. No one knew what had happened then or afterwards. All they really knew was that she followed him to the Fair and then they had gone out in the country with a lunch and then she had been found lying in that shed, with her umbrella and a new hat with a red ribbon on it beside her. Either she had shot herself or Hawk had shot her. Miss Shelley never said what happened. No one had heard her say much about it at all when it came right down to it.

Everyone would tell you about how her jacket was lying south of her head, that she had only her last petticoat on, that her skirt had been spread on the ground, as if for a bed, that her umbrella, of all things with a hawk's head on it, had been lying west of the cross timber or was it east? near the front of the shed; and had it been blood the engineer had seen from the five-thirty express to Kansas City or had it been that red ribbon on her hat? Some of the women said they had a piece of that red ribbon but I never saw any of it. Some said Miss Shelley had the umbrella and the hat to this day. But she never showed it. I never saw it.

Afterwards, of course, she couldn't get a school anywhere. Even if the tale had not followed her, she carried it like a guilt, like a child she might have gotten, that would never be born out of her, but would die and rot and eat off her until she was dead. Her family had kept her within itself. She had scarcely gone out of the house, until her father and mother died leaving her alone in the house on Maple Street.

So she had taken to living off what happened to other people as best she could. And the Town lived off what had happened to her. Men enjoyed their wives more and their own loss lay in her and the mutilations they gave each other.

And I, a young girl then, the same as she had been before, saw the way it went, beauty having two ways, disaster, then change, one way or another.

The day I went to Nina Shelley's to make fudge she
had asked Cora Little, too; and we both went in together
and Cora kept giggling and nudging me and I felt embarrassed and opened my eyes wide and looked straight at
Miss Shelley as she opened the door a crack showing her
bony nose and one eye; and the shadows of the house then
reared up behind her as she opened and we came into the
musty dark, seeing the empty chairs and the hand–tinted
pictures of her dead mother and father on the wall.

We followed her swishing skirts just seeing her
walking primly in front of us but I could feel she was
excited and when she turned to let us pass her in the
doorway into the kitchen, I could see her eyes glinting and
her thin discolored hand shook. I wondered why she liked
young girls to come there to make fudge of all things.

But the kitchen was clean and bright, the sun coming
in from the back yard, and we could see the green grass,
and the way we went to school down past the gravel pit. So
we felt better.

"Well, here we are," Miss Shelley said, laughing girl-
ishly and looked at us as if she fed off us or was expecting
some rare pleasure of us. I had too an impression I remember that she might want to deal us some blow. I
remember I thought quite distinctly, she may want to kill
us. I was confused but I remember I knew then that she
had asked us there for a purpose and that she asked every
young girl there for the same purpose. And it was certainly
much more than making fudge.

We weren't much good. Cora stood holding her
elbows and kind of giggling and I dropped the mixing bowl
so Miss Shelley laughed and began mixing herself, talking
in a light girlish voice all the time.

It didn't seem long before the fudge was on the stove
just beginning to boil. It was quick because none of us
was thinking about the fudge. We were waiting for
something. Only Miss Shelley knew what it was.

We sat down by the kitchen table to wait for the fudge
to boil and Miss Shelley got a cup of cold water ready to
test it and set it beside her. The afternoon sun came in the
window and struck on Cora, and I could see the golden
hairs on her arms which she put on the table still holding
her elbows in her hands, and it fell on the dead rats puffed
high over the thin hair of Miss Shelley who sat between us
and she kept looking first at Cora and then at me in a
terrible excitement. And her red tongue kept licking out
over her lips as if her tongue was the only thing left in her

with blood in it.   And then I remember she leaned over, looking quickly at both of us, her tongue going out over her mouth, and said, her eyes glinting up from her dried skin, "My, I seen a sight in this Town during my time. My, I could tell you a mite."

I could see Cora just gripping her arms and looking down and I could see Miss Shelley's hands gripping the sides of the kitchen chair, her body rigid with some kind of vindictive power that came out of her, as vigor or beauty might come from another.   "I seen a sight all right," she said, licking her lips.

Then Cora said, clearing her throat twice and speaking huskily, as if out of politeness more than anything, "What have you seen?"

Miss Shelley opened her eyes full upon us so they showed green in the center, "I seen what was happening to everybody in this Town. I know a heap I don't tell. I suppose you've heard a lot about me, some is right and some is wrong. But I know a heap too. I can tell a heap when I want to."

And I heard myself saying, "Why do you have to tell it?"   I was frightened.

"Why do I have to tell it?"   Miss Shelley kind of lifted her sharp shoulders and said, "Ha," in a way that made it wrench the cords of her neck out and stretch her mouth and dilate her nose. "Ha," she said, "I got plenty on this Town too. I been sittin' here. I got a sight."

Cora was cracking her knuckles. "I better test the fudge," she said half getting up but Miss Shelley said, "You set down. I know to a minute when it's done."   And she leaned forward as if she had been waiting for that moment and I saw how no part of her flowed together with any ease, but every articulation held a tension of hate that made it a wonder she was ever taken in any rest and I knew something awful had happened to her and I didn't want to hear what it was. And yet I knew if she started telling it I would have to listen even though I never heard another thing all my life after that. And it would make the taste of everything bitter.

"Why do you have to tell it?" I said and I felt as if I had shouted it out.

"I got my reasons," Miss Shelley said drumming on the table and looking out the window with absolutely blind eyes; and I looked out too where she should have been looking; and then suddenly I knew, as if someone had told me, that Miss Shelley had not really looked out that window since the Thing had happened. A chill crept in the roots of my hair and my feet were dead at the ends of my legs and my hands sweated and I thought I'd never be able to live if I heard what had really happened to her and I felt that I was going to get up and scream right there, "Don't tell us. Let us alone. Maybe it won't happen to us too. Let us alone . . ."

But just then the candy rose, hissing on the fire.

We were sitting in the back yard then waiting for the fudge to get hard and Miss Shelley was sitting on the ground like a young coquettish teacher with her legs pulled up under her skirt and I could see plainly that time on her when her body was young and long, when she would be sitting looking with pleasure at what was happening at a picnic or a party. I could see her almost like some part of myself but the ruthless sun made her look like a caricature of that time and that perfection and showed her up like a rotten piece of wood.

Cora sat on the other side of her still scrooched over herself as if she thought Miss Shelley was going to hit her in the stomach and I kept plucking blades of grass and sliding them through my teeth but I was shaking and my hands and feet were numb because I knew she was going to tell us and nothing could stop her.

And sure enough she began: "You know I expect you've heard people say plenty about me," she said smoothing down her old dress with her ghastly bony fingers and looking up at us beneath her brows and smiling with her bloodless mouth. "You see," she said, "I almost got married one time."

Cora and I looked at each other.

"Well," Miss Shelley went on bending her head sideways just as she must have as a girl but now she looked strange as if one thing slid across another like a film double exposed. I remember I felt sick and my pity and dread went over the old woman. "Yes, Miss Shelley," I said.

"Oh, it ain't much," she said raising her hand stiffly.

"I wouldn't think on it," Cora said in a small voice bending down over her arms and looking at the grass.

"It's this way, girls," Miss Shelley went on and we looked at her knowing now we must hear what it was and nothing could keep us from hearing. "You see I don't speak of it much, I don't think such things should be spoken of. They're too sacred." She set her lips so they

didn't show at all and looked over our heads. I kept letting
the green blade slide between my lips but I knew my pity
was ready to flow over what we were about to hear and I
waited thinking the least I could do was to let it fall in a
space of quiet and be mute.

"Yes, Miss Shelley," I said again.

"Well," she said unexpectedly, "I feel my life has
been very, very beautiful." She let her head fall to one
side, the big rats shifting on her head. "Very beautiful,"
she said softly, letting her dead voice fall down as if it lay
far below the sunlight like something under an old board.
She spoke like a ghost so the immediate air was still around
her, as if she did not live in our summer, but was echoing
some lost time, like some fermented decaying thing, rising
filling every moment, its fumes usurping the present entirely. "Very beautiful," she said again. Her eyes closed dra-
matically.

Some delicacy made us look away. Cora looked as if
she was trying to forget all about Miss Shelley and what she
was saying but I knew she was listening to every word.

"You see I was engaged to marry Hawk. Yes, he was
a member of one of the best families in town, that's a fact.
Well, we had a lovely courtship. Nobody in this Town can
say different." She waited. The maple shook. Cora and I
were listening thinking of what might happen to us when
something would begin happening.

"Yes, it was one of the most beautiful things. He was
so tender, so courteous. A woman could not want a more
tender courtship, I often say. It was too perfect, yes, I
often said to my mother, too perfect."

I lowered my head remembering what I had heard men
saying, women saying, seeing then in my mind's eye three
things, what had been said about it, what it had become in
Miss Shelley's mind, fusing together, lapping over, and
then there was a terrific thing stood up beside me between
that old woman and myself — *What had really happened?*

I don't remember the words. I know I was sitting
cramped, not daring to move; knowing I was looking upon
something awful, as Miss Shelley, in her lisping voice, now
becoming shadowed so that you might have been fooled
into thinking it was the voice of the young Miss Shelley
before *it* had happened, her eyes lowered in proper
modesty, told how they had decided their love was too
pure, too perfect for this world . . . more like the love of
Christ for the church . . . that was what she said, and that it

must not be spoiled by mundane things into the poor life
they saw all about them, that it must remain that high pure
thing unsullied by passion. "You understand, girls, I
trust," she said as if she were reading from an invisible
book she held in her hand. "You understand, I trust," she
said, looking at the round downy arms of Cora Little and
at my own long hungering body with contempt. She flung
up her neck, hanging in dead pouches and I knew that to
her it was slim and lovely as a swan's, that her lips fouled
by that shadow were once fair and parted and for a
moment we saw the resurrection by this fantasy of her dead
self, as if it could last.

"Well I remember that summer day," she said, her
smile ghastly on her slanting face, "Mr. Hawk came and
we drove right through the Town, a proud couple we were.
I remember the very dress I wore, and the new parasol
papa brought from Kansas City that matched." Cora and
I looked at each other. Could that have been the very
parasol found beside her when she was found shot? "It
was on that day Mr. Hawk proposed to me. I remember it
as if it was yesterday. Yes . . . yes. . . . We stopped down
by the creek. He was a romantic one, you know, and going
down on his knees he says . . ." She stopped.

"Yes, Miss Shelley," I said in agony. I knew then she
must be lying. Cora was smiling evilly behind her hand
and I was afraid Miss Shelley would see it. But she wasn't
seeing anything in *that* afternoon.

"Yes . . . yes . . ." she said, "yes, well I remember it
like it was yesterday. I do for a fact. And I said no. Loving him like I did, girls, I said no because I didn't want
such a love sullied. That's just the word I used, sullied. We
drove back in the gloaming, very slow. It was beautiful. . . ."

Neither of us could look straight at her. There was a
stillness as if Miss Shelley had stepped off into a vacuum
where we could not follow, beyond that afternoon's sun.
She had her head tilted, that idiotic smile was stretching
her lips as if she sat now, her bones showing, the skin
raveled, under that tiny umbrella amidst her ruffles, beside
Hawk that far afternoon. I shivered right in the sun
because it was like some terrible magic that Miss Shelley
had aged and shriveled but still sat preserved like some
body in a tomb, in that afternoon twenty years before
under an absurd umbrella, expecting something to happen.

Then I saw Cora getting up and I saw that grin on her face that nearly everyone had when they talked or thought about Miss Shelley. I knew she was going to say something awful. I didn't want her to say it. 'See if the fudge is ready to eat,'' I said to her but I couldn't stop her. She flaunted her skirts around her legs that were more developed than mine and made her seem mature.

"What happened to Hawk," she said pulling down her dress over her full bosom that the girls all envied.

"Hawk? My dear," Miss Shelley said like a great lady. "He has become a great financier. Yes, he changed his name," she said quickly. "No one knows it but myself. And once a year I receive a gorgeous present from him. But I trust all this is between only us." She was very gentle now from her imagined world, for an earth lost in sin, unwilling to be saved, doomed to its own sullied evil.

But I wanted to cry out. "But what really happened? What was it? Warn us. Save us. Nobody tells us anything. You all know something and you don't tell us. . . . What people say isn't so. You'll all go to hell if you don't tell . . . if you don't save us from dying too."

But I didn't say it. I didn't know how. And we all got up and went in to look at the fudge which was just for that afternoon. Nobody ate much except Cora who was still smiling as if she knew something and I was afraid she was going to hurt Miss Shelley more, and I kept wanting to really ask her so my throat ached. I couldn't have swallowed the fudge if some one had paid me.

Cora said wickedly, "I've got to go." And she walked out very boldly, her skirts flicking around her legs where they curved out at the calf and it made me feel I would never be able to leave, that I could not get away as if some evil had spun a web around me so I could not move in any direction. We stood at the screen door watching Cora sway her hips down the green lawn; then I saw her stop, turn and beckon to me. I always did everything Cora told me because of the way her legs and bosom went; and so I stood close to her, smelling that perfume she used, and she began to whisper in my ear. At first I couldn't hear. I could see Miss Shelley still standing in the doorway.

Then I heard quite distinctly what Cora was whispering. "Ask Miss Shelley," she said, "if it was her loving suitor shot her!" Laughing she went down the bank, around the house to the street. "Ta-ta," she called. I stood looking at the grass.

"What did she say?" Miss Shelley called in her cracking voice.

"I don't know," I said miserably, "I don't know. I couldn't hear her."

The sun beat down between us and now that we were alone everything the woman was seemed painfully to flow into me, into all the parts of me where nothing had as yet happened and I was no longer myself but the woman I might become and the tortured woman standing in the door not three feet away kept threading through me like a taut wire that hummed and moved in my flesh.

"You must take some fudge," I heard her say. And that afternoon the earth, the sun, the summer air seemed to have in it something that was not for human beings in that Town, as if it did not fall on them so they stayed green and forbidding with never a good taste of ripe fruit. I wanted to start running and never come back but I thought of the endless prairies and knew that I would only come to another Town exactly like this one.

"You must take some fudge," she called out from the kitchen and I heard her cracking voice cold and drear,

> "In the sweet by and by
> We shall meet on that beautiful shore . . . ."

I didn't run, and in that moment I cracked the meaning in my teeth and the bitterness of it lay in me then, and I had to say it. In that moment I faced *it*, what had been coiling around the thought of Miss Shelley, what had been approaching, almost seen then gone; what had stood behind all the facts, everything men had been saying and women had been saying, so that what had happened became large, vent for their poisons. Now it all came from behind what had stood before it and I had to let my lips come over it and know it forever with what I would be able to find out about other things.

She had had a hunger just like me and that day they talk about when she was going and going after Hawk and they saw her riding towards the orchard in her new dress under her little umbrella, then she couldn't do it. She couldn't do it. She couldn't know. She couldn't risk. She wasn't able, that's what, she wasn't able. What nobody was knowing, what was standing in that Town over Miss Shelley's house was that nothing happened. Nothing happened! Except the wound that she gave to herself, taking a shot at her own breast. And the Town's rancor standing equally in them all was that nothing happened in any of them, neither sun, moon, husband, or child broke them open to good growing.

And I remember that standing in the sun I began to cry as if for my own lost life that had not yet begun and yet stood finished before me.

"Take some fudge," cried Miss Shelley peering from the door. "Take some fudge to your mother."

Autumnal Village

Why should he have to go out, now the summer is going, and shoot at the bright pheasants? I went as far as the spring with him this morning, and there were little cries of birds in the brush and our feet in the dead leaves, and I stood beside his lean body with the stooping head and the delicate pointed nose, and what has happened to me now that my love is a ghost, that the disaster of the Fall makes my blood fall in bitter cascade?

He looked at me coldly, with the leaves dropping around us. Are you sure you don't want to go? he said. I looked away to the hills and the village, now half exposed from their summer lushness so you could see the white spires of the churches and the brightly colored earth. No, I said, and saw the children running out of the house, calling down the hill.

He leaned over a little and I started back from the thin peck of his kiss. He stood a moment with his thin jowls close to me and I stood still so he would not find me out. Then he went down the hill with the Winchester through his arm and did not look back.

For a moment I felt like crying out and I stood holding my arms across my breast and the children came running in the wind behind me, crying, Mama — Mama, and then the two girls came eddying round my skirts, their hands upreaching and their cries like a confusion of birds, flying off into the autumnal air, around my head.

But when he was out of sight I forgot about him and walked up the hill to the great house he had built, not for me, but for his position, for the looks of it in the world, for the bargains he would be making because of it. O, it was a buckle to wear on his belt — the house, the children, and myself in fine clothes — a feather in his cap and bitter gall in my own mouth.

What could be happening between one moment and the next to change the heart in a woman? Here we are, it is Fall, and the leaves falling, the bare trees and the warm, still golden and green hills, the russet oaks and the terribly blue sky, the frail golden-light sliver of the tan grasses, slanting down the stems the way it does in the fall. The summer nests are now visible, hanging like pouches from the branches. Everything seems close — the trees are closer to the house — the road is closer and the hills move up. The train in the valley is nearer. Next summer is white upon the bough already. In death everything opens a little to reveal itself. There is the heavy smell of smoke and apples and wine.

Such a small thing to turn the tide of the blood completely. If my brother hadn't taken the car perhaps it would never have happened at all. It is nice to walk but you never do it if you have a car, you only do it when there is no car, and then you like it. Before this I couldn't sit down in any peace, take a walk, give the children a bath or enjoy the thick smooth surface of the world.

After he left we could see him walking down the hills to the ferry and afterwards hear the soft ping of his rifle on the hills that were his private preserve — where the signs read over the forest — *PRIVATE. No Trespassing.*

Now, after the bright day, the night is alive with sound. He has not come back from hunting. If he comes I feel I will have to hide in the darkness away from him.

After he left, the morning was like newly washed linen with little birds painted on it, and we walked to the village, Marya and Ruth running ahead to pick berries. The village is about a mile, and it was a pleasure to be walking in the thin bright stream of cold fall air that made your cheeks cold and fine, like the cheeks of an apple. Marya and Ruth ran ahead and then back again, as if the bright thread of autumnal space tethered them to me, giving them only a space to run and pulling them back again to touch me with their bright faces lifted, the blood mounting and falling in their fat cheeks.

Marya would walk straight and single, her black bob swinging like a bell around the tiny clapper of her face, and Ruth a little stouter and more solid on the earth, setting her fat legs straight down, her round face like some ripe fruit hanging in the air; and crying out, they both were, with the pleasure of it all, and how it was better than the city, with frogs looking out from the brush, birds above you in the sky and snakes quick into the goldenrod as you walk.

Farm women were gathering fagots against the winter. They are sad but strong, walking and stooping slowly. They have nothing to can this year. Women stand at their doors. The tomatoes are no good so there is no piccalilli. I feel young and yet heavy. It is bad to feel the sadness and disgrace of one's own body, bloated with grief.

We turned the corner by the cedar, walking away from the river that looked as if it would flow on forever, full and bright. There lay the village with its tiny white houses and church spires like an old Flemish painting, amid the bare strong trees; and there in the doorway of the Rankins' house sat Mrs. Rankin offering her rosy nipple to the stout baby and Mr. Rankin standing beside her holding out a dish of apples. Their faces lifted to see who would be passing and the children slowed down, turning their heads to see the great mounds of the woman offering her white globe of breast to the eager child. We nod silently to each other without speaking and we can feel their candid gaze against our backs, and we are hurried along as if pushed with unwelcome.

Marya and Ruth wait at the post office standing back from the old odòr of two ancient men who like crickets are leaning on their crooked legs, chirping in the doorway. I thought you were dead and buried long ago, said one to the other, and he answered in a high voice, I'll be around a long time after you're gone and measured all your length upon the sod.

The other said, You'll have to go a long way in time to beat me pardner. I aim to live a mighty long time from now. And they bent to each other, all their labors marked upon the turn of bone and the rot of flesh, like some half gay emissaries of death.

They looked from rheumy eyes at the passing of the children as they drew in like colts close to my flanks; feeling the hostile eye and turned shoulder of the village. We asked for the mail and there was none, and edged out past the two old men with the mark of their work like a signature upon their skin; and I felt ashamed of my heavy flesh and the useless weight of my grief, now heavy as autumn on my bones.

We went softly down the dirt road and we seemed to be listening to all the sounds of cry-to-horse and oath-at-labor, and the sawing of the winter wood in the forest before the men came home to lunch. We drew together, excluded from the common labors, conscious of their silent stare upon our backs. Why are we intruders now who own it all, the mills, the land, the seed. I felt like curious apology. . . . *If I am walking with my children, listening to the mouthings of ancient men, what is it to you? If I am walking, a woman, proud, unhusbanded, my flesh badly harvested as your land, in fresh wound and new*

*lesion, do you look upon me in grief too? I am walking on
this pillaged land too, and bear the brunt of those hunters
who have ravaged it. I am walking over this bridge, with
the thighs of the hills alive and the milk from the breast of
the wind, and a yearning with you to be alive and a long
way from measuring my height upon the sod.*

The soft sharp ping of the shots from the hunters falls
metallic against the hills, ricochets back and is killed by the
wind.

I feel again the dire and black shame of his lean kiss as
he hung like a knife above me, with the Winchester on his
arm.

The sharp ping of the shot comes from the hills.

We walked too far in the strong earth-day. Our
basket was full and the children full of the cold tang and
sleep. The echoes of the shots kept breaking across the
river, against the hills and then around the naked bowl,
from the waters and the earth.

We sat on a giant tree body, split down the center.
Half of it was standing. We looked up at the white meat
exposed and hardened. I said, the other half of it will fall.
Marya said, is it old as Father? I said, it is much older.
She looked at it, into the white bark split by lightning on
some dark night. It will fall, she said.

We were just walking, not taking any heed, going
under fences. Sometimes the shots of the hunters seemed
so close I was afraid we might be shot. But children in
bright dresses from the village went in droves through the
bare trunked trees and the cows began to go slowly in to be
milked and the sun went down steadily towards the south-
west slightly shrouded in smoke and haze. Marya and
Ruth walked ahead and the shadows of the earth moved
steadily eastward and we walked into them as into dark
water.

The children felt this, standing straight and no bigger
than little saplings on the edge of darkening shadow.
Look, Marya said, pointing to the down slope of a
meadow now darkening, the dark lathing down its side.
The bright dark, she said, and it did look so bright and at
the same time so dark. There was the strange death
glimmer of the Fall with this ghostly light. I lifted my head
to the pure frail light and saw Ruth and Marya standing, a
dark thin stroke in the light, pointing to the growing
shadow.

And suddenly, without warning, the sky looked like a bursting purple grape and the wind came out of a cloud like an explosion, and the trees looked like women trying to run with their hair flying, and the dark earth seemed to rear towards the sun and the black mane of earth rearing and running, with black foliage like blood from a horse's mouth and the full-to-bursting clouds. I felt a cry from my throat.

Someone shot from the lake. I took the children's hands and we started to run, falling down in the peaty bog. We climbed a fence and got to the road. We seemed defenseless. I felt I had never seen a road before like this, with only my two feet to take me down it. I couldn't recognize anything moving and tearing at its roots like this. We stood in the road and a little rain fell cold on us and then stopped, and we could hardly root ourselves in the road, the wind was so sudden-strong.

Before we knew it an old Ford stopped and two men were looking from their beards at us asking us to get in, and one got out and put out his hands and with one paw around their tiny ribs lifted Marya and Ruth to the back seat, and I found myself between the two men who smelled of oats and sweat.

Then the rain began to come down fast and the road to steam and the dry fields took it in. The two men looked out the steaming windows and lifted the old side curtains. Holy Christopher, they spoke in round and hearty words to celebrate the rain, and the smell from their caked clothes came out like sour buttermilk and the hands of the big man driving were like huge horned toads, and once we nearly turned around on the wet pavement and I could feel the children's eyes upon my back and knew they would be sitting still and straight, in homage to their own fright and to the terror of the world.

We went past farm and school grateful in the rain with faces pressed to windows, and women running to bring in the clothes, and sudden as it began it stopped and the sky looked like a wet bright stone. There was the rich glisten and turn of wet skin and feather. And the two men peered out with wonder at the passing storm, sticking out wet fingers to test the wind and speaking in a strange language of fallow field and rich, of rainfall, of winter, of the way it was so cold in March the lambing was no good, the seed barely came from the ground, and burnt were the rest entirely.

Will you ma'am, the driver said to me, the first words
he had said to me, would you mind if we stopped in here at
Ed Mason's for only a second, to find out if he has any
feed he would be lending until our loans come in. Why no,
I said, of course, and we drove up a bare slope of ground
and stopped in the yard beside a bare frame house. A
blonde woman and five children came to the door and a
young farmer came around the barn. Some rain, they said,
and nodded; and the men stood together talking and the
woman and I looked at each other shyly and the children
looked at the towheads and not a word was spoken but
suddenly, like the rain, I felt happy and wanted to speak to
the woman but I said nothing and the men walked back to
the car paying no attention to us, lean as hounds upon their
man problems. And I felt good for the moment and sat
still and the men were laughing and the two big ones got
into the car and still talked, saying that the Russian thistle
was not such shakes for a cow, that it made her milk bad in
a little while, with no butter, and that two years of drouth
like this made the flesh bad in such a way that it was no
good again to fatten it up, that the flesh was gone for good
then and you had to breed it over if you wanted your herd
A-1 again.

And the talk went on and I was sitting between the two
farmers, feeling their strong thighs and the strong caked
clothes and the great bearded faces so close to me with the
powerful words like talons, and I felt full of wonder,
looking at the lean farm woman standing there without
introduction, and the children, and why was I outside the
heart of this real happening? And then I knew that they
knew the land my husband owned so they could walk it in
the dark, and see a hill that they had seeded and stood in to
the waist, and the women knowing the earth as close as a
bed quilt to the hand. I felt my eyes open on a world I
never knew. We got one lone mule, they said, to cultivate
and the soil has been dry as a contribution box. Poor luck
this year and that's a fact. Dry weather in the farrowing
season, cold weather during lambing, and then they
shipped the grass-fat weathers from Texas, putting down
the price of our meat. It's a crying shame, they said, and
the feed is higher and the prices lower, they said, and the
corn is poor and seed is none too plentiful in the feed belt
and the number of cattle on feed is pretty small. It's a poor
year. It's a bad year. Well we gotta be going, we got to be
on our way . . .

And the engine started, the woman raised her hand simply and I sat there dumb, the children waved and at the sound of the motor the red hens ran toward the barn like old women with their skirts lifted.

Where do you live they said, and I didn't want them to know I was *his* wife because they talked so bitterly about the mill being shut, so I said I'd get out at the bottom of the hill and they thought it peculiar but they let me out and one of them lifted the children out again and set them on the still-wet road. Thank you very much, I said, and I bowed to them. They took off their hats then and I was confused and felt the blood mount to my cheeks and I backed away and we half stumbled up the hill to the house. The rain fell off the great plumed trees heavy with their past living and their coming death. It fell on us and I took the children's hands and we started to run. *O you are wild young daughters* I cried to them, feeling my breast drive deep as the soil *O what wild young daughters!* And they began running and crying out shrilly and laughing . . .

There is the long hoot of the train. It sounds different on fall nights than it does in summer. In the summer it was like a festival coming through the green foliage, over the bright hills. Now it sounds like something sharp in the frosty night. The antlered trees are like black nerves jutting the thick earth. I can see the spring at the bottom of the hill where I left him this morning.

O what is the inordinate and terrible desire for physical life, the forest, the garden, the gentians the tiny bright hepaticas, the rain, hail, lightning, thunder, the wonderful flashing on the body of the earth, the day on the river, the children wonderful-solid, the bearded farmers, the wild dark-crusted earth like a grape.

You might get so filled up in the day with red hens running like old women with their skirts lifted, and two farmers with round quick eyes and a strong, strong brogue and the fog rising to fall upon us later in rain O he had a strong brogue to him, the one who drove, and what with the longing and the hunger in me he was like the sight of the hills and the fog rising and the wild turkeys walking strong and gentle up the saffron slope. O he had a strong male brogue to him, pointing out his precious bull standing with his cows looking out of the pearly fog, and his soft cows around him, so gentle, rolling a gentle round eye and loping gently with their swinging bags.

What puts such a fierceness in a man that when you see it you forget you've been without it? What puts such strong fierce marrow in a man that makes your breast ache inside your vaulted ribs to hear him barking out with laughter from his barrel chest that you couldn't be spanning with both arms. What gives him such strength in the day, such a brawny stance looking over the turkeys like a lord of creation himself?

The soft delicate little hills lying prone across the sky and the black dying trees like the beards on their chins, and them shaking their manes and their good eyes looking on the world of flesh and wheat and seed.

And running up the hill afterwards with Marya and Ruth, past the houses where farmers parted curtains to watch us pass, up the dark crest of rising mountain. We went running and crying out to each other, my children and I, and the hills were cold with coming winter and far ahead was the blue and lonely sky.

And the soft ping of hunters that I could not see, from the brush.

He is coming up the dark hill now. He will come in the front hall. He will lift up the limp bodies of the rabbits and show me how he caught them square between the eyes, and the bright bodies of male and female pheasants with shot in the breast and their necks hanging broken and their eyes half open in the voluptuous death he loves. He will be a knife leaning above me as he kisses me.

God Made Little Apples

"Yeah . . . yeah," Lars said. "Arrested . . . well, I'll be —"

"What is it?" the women clattered from the kitchen like geese.

Lord . . . so many women he had! He saw their fair fat flesh steaming in the morning kitchen, with the broth and coffee. "Well," he said, "what do you know? The old devil. That's the way for a man to act now after harvest."

"What is it?" Helga, his wife, said, turning her bright face. And the wizened face of his mother looked over the coffee pot, and there were the round laughing faces of his three big girls.

"It's Grandpa," Emily, the oldest, said. "Oh, Grandpa has spent his harvest money."

"Oh," Grandma said, "that old codger!"

"Yas," Lars said, swatting his huge thigh, "yas, the old man's in jail in Hastings — smack in jail and wants me to come get him out. There's a man for you. First harvest in four years and there goes the harvest money! Ho, ho, ha, ha!"

"Tch, tch, tch!" Grandma said, but she couldn't help smiling.

"Now, Helga, you'd have some complaining to do proper if I did that in the fall. It's a fair day for deviltry. Got a mind to go after him and stop and see Mrs. Potter I courted forty years ago, and would have married her, too."

"Gone on!" Helga said, flicking him with a towel.

"Tell us, Pa . . ."

"You're too young," he laughed, listening to the clucks, the warm talk of the women. He thought, "One good season can make a man feel good. Haven't been across the river for years. Wonder what Effie Potter looks like now; she used to be a sweet apple-faced gal for certain. Suppose I had married her." But he looked at Helga, warm as bread, opulent as his fields this year, mother of his seven children. No drouth in her.

And now the land, the weather, was with you again; the barn was full of hay.

"I'll go with you," Helga said. "The canning's done;
I haven't had a vacation . . ."

He didn't know why he was set against her going. He
wanted to get away from her, from them all.

"I'll get my things and go along," Grandma said. "I
know how to handle these things. Every year at harvest . . ."

"No, you don't!" Lars said. "This is a man's affair.
I think I'll join the old coot for a nip."

"Lars!" Helga said, and he saw her anxious eyes, blue
as his mother's, and the great braids wound on her head,
white now, as the snow of Sweden. "Mama," Helga said,
"have you got the harvest money?"

"No," the old lady said, grinning in her empty gums,
"he's the man of the family . . ."

"Twice a year," Helga said, "all his life, roaring
drunk at seeding, at harvest!"

"You see what I tell you," Lars said, "you don't
appreciate me."

"Lars," Helga said, "you're spoiled."

"How will we get him out?" the old lady said.

"I'll go get him out; I'll go this very morning. The
cows are milked; the haying's done," And he thought, "I
can go across the river. Why, I haven't driven over there in
nearly forty years. I haven't seen Effie since her wedding
day . . ."

He felt caught inside his life, inside the warm kitchen,
in the golden hair of his women, his six girls. And he felt
enormous, like a man who has been sweating at fighting in
too small a space, a six-room house, ninety acres, where
you plowed your sweat, and thought, riding all day on the
sand, that it was like the fine hair of your Scandinavian
women. Suddenly, he was greatly excited.

He rose in his chair, roaring for his good shirt, his
Sunday shirt. "Iron it!" he cried, and stood in the kitchen
roaring.

The women scampered like geese when he roared like
that. He had on his clean shirt . . . Helga cut his hair
around the edges . . . he pared his big nails.

"You're dressing up like your wedding day," Helga
twitted.

"Might meet a brace of apple-cheeked gals," he
laughed, and she made a face at him.

Then he got into the car, without a pig to market,
without a bag of grain, free to cross the river into the fair,

fall, country hills. Tiny villages, bearing the mark of men like himself who had come from his own country, seamen like his ancestors, with fierce scarred faces, tight curls and earrings.

He looked back and saw the girls waving, saw Helga by the door, and her kiss had meant, Do not get drunk. For a moment he wondered what is it — good year, bad years, your life, the sun shining down, women's faces laughing, a picture of your mother in a full skirt, mortgages making a ghost of the spoons you ate off? He waved, and turned the car down the road towards the river, through the village, across the bridge, up the river road and seemed to be driving into his childhood, his mother beside him, as she clucked to the horses and held him loose in her great skirts so he wouldn't fall. In the tiny mirror of the Ford he laughed, roared with laughter, seeing his thick pelt of a neck and one eye looking from the burned laps of skin pitted like the sand from his own hills; and the eye kept looking at him and made him laugh.

Memory lay like a thick mosaic all around him, a substance sweet and heavy. The wrecked and ruined houses, and the shapes of the strong men who had lived in them, thirty years before. There was the house of Strawberry Pratt, one of the first lumbermen. The house was empty now and the shutters flapping. The sawmills gone, the villages removed, a few white houses looking like New England, and some summer tourists. You passed cars with canoes on top and motorboats in trailers, and summer bedding and cookstoves piled in them. All along the river the old men stooped in the melon patches. And there was the store of old Sam. He could beat you out of your mother-in-law. By Heavens, he remembered the time Sam beat him out of a fighting cock, and he came away without the cock and with a couple of old hens not worth the powder to blow them up! Old Sam was dead now.

As he drove into the lift of the hills toward Effie's he thought he remembered certain trees, turns in the road, and a curious excitement made him drive faster. Her husband was dead now and she lived alone on the hill, her son gone away. He saw the barns empty. What harm was there in going to see Effie? Yet he looked down the road to see if anyone was behind him. An old collie came out to meet him after he had passed the windmill and the cream house, and a big rooster strutted past the wheels, and Lars laughed as if he had nothing to do but go traipsing around the country visiting old loves.

When he stood by the door looking into the cool, dark summer kitchen, flavorsome, smelling of piccalilli, and — did he imagine it? — the lavender perfume Effie used to use, he grinned sheepishly to feel his heart hammering as he waited for an answer to his knock. But he wasn't prepared for the woman who strode from the darkness, peering at him through the sunlight as if from the grave. She was wearing an old hat and the face of Effie as he remembered her hung like a dream in the layers of old flesh.

"What do you want?" she said, peering blindly, and the dead bird, hanging with dead claws to the hat, seemed to see him more brightly.

"Howdy," Lars said, and knew that she didn't remember him nor ever would. She giggled and thrust the hat on her rats, and he smelled beer on her breath. "I thought maybe you had a calf to sell."

"No," she said, "the barn is empty. I tell you —" She went on with the garrulousness of people who live alone, as if continuing a conversation she had been having many years in a lonely house with herself. 'I tell you I got my troubles. Did my only son have a right to leave his poor old mother?"

He stood awkwardly in the door, the sun shining on his back, and the odorous dark out of which the old woman loomed going over him like a litany of disaster, over everything that she had lost, remembering every lost thing, stove, chickens, child, husband, chair, cow, bird; taken by flood, famine, cholera, graft, or natural decay and rot. Her mind was like a huge and fabulous junkyard filled with the idiocy of inanimate things to be lost, maimed, forgotten, ruined, until he could stand it no longer. But she didn't want him to go now, seeing his hungry startled listening, and she followed him to the car, clinging to its side, thrusting her ruined face at him.

And when he drove away, leaving her on the stone threshold still counting up disasters, he felt sick and wanted a drink, and drove away fast to Sam's tavern and drank down two cool draughts of beer, before he felt good again, and bought two hot melons which he thought he would eat for lunch. The day was bright, lying under the prismatic glass of sky, and the blue mist fell in the shadows of the stacks and followed each fattening Thanksgiving turkey, and he filled his pipe and began to laugh, thinking of the old man in the cooler.

Afton was a village named by Scotsmen. It was a
nice neat village with cows grazing in the lowlands by the
river, an old hotel he had known as a child, little farms and
neat English houses. Many of these people had been
seamen like his own, had come at the same time, but he
didn't know them or they him. Only ten miles from his
house and he didn't know them from Adam. He had a
feeling for going in and asking them, "What do you know?
How do you find it?? What's up? How's tricks?" What
would you say? "Well, I've been living for sixty years ten
miles from you. Ain't it time we got acquainted?"

He stopped at the lunchroom and sat on a stool. An
old woman came down the steps from the kitchen. She
said in a queer voice, "What do you want?" and it
sounded as if it were coming from a throat caught in a
noose. He looked at her and saw where her whole throat
had been burned, shooting right up beneath her eyes. She
brought him some homemade cake and whipped cream,
and he ate, wondering how it would go with the beer. And
he still felt hungry, but he paid her, said good day, and
went out. The village street lay quiet, empty. He got into
the car and took to the road that went now into the hills, a
dirt road, lined with birches and grapevines and gold and
purple flowers of harvest blooming, goldenrod and gravel
root.

He drove along slowly, smoking, putting one foot up
on the door to cool it off; the lizzy got pretty warm on the
hills. He drove slowly because of the love he had for
looking at all the tiny farms on the hills, seeing the grains
all cut, the corncribs full, everything looking neat; but he
could see how they clung to the hills by the skin of their
teeth, too. He could read the farms like a book. It was
very interesting as he went along. He could see the signs of
struggle. "Bees . . . now they are trying bees," he thought;
"they think they'll make out with bees." Then someone
had tried raising peanuts. "You can't do that here," he
thought; "they'll find that out." And ducks and musk-
rats.

He knew how it was:

Always reading in some journal how if you got this or
that you'd be sitting in clover, all your troubles over,
everything hunky-dory. He'd done it himself, put in this
and that, pulled it out, found the soil or the climate no
good for it, that it was a racket. Ah, it was a fine thing to
look at the farms when they had half a chance, when there

was half a crop, and half a price. The animals looked
good, too, and he passed trucks full of squealing fat hogs
going to market, and saw the faces of heifers and steers
looking over the laths. He stopped once and some sheep
came to the fence and looked at him, and he looked at
them. He knew the hills would be full of berries and
grapes, but he felt too lazy to get them. He had done his
harvesting. He thought he would bring the girls down
some day and let them gather grapes and berries, but he
knew he never would.

He stopped at another tavern at the crossroads, where
an old man with a dog gave him beer, the dog walking at
the old man's heels. He drank down the beer and had
another. He didn't count the money spent. He was like a
man at a carnival who will cheerfully spend everything he
has. The old man sat down with him after the fifth beer
and had one himself, and they both lighted up and talked
about crops, the fishing, and the weather. And then they
got to telling stories.

They both laughed and their pipes went out, and they
lighted up again, and the old man brought two more beers
and told another story. They laughed and looked out the
window down the road where two carloads of fishermen
were just coming up from the river, their poles on top of
their cars. And the old man began to tell about when he
was young, and Lars listened and it seemed pretty
wonderful to him. And the old man got out some pictures
in an old cigar box that had a picture of a chorus girl of the
Nineties stuck on the lid; and he showed Lars pictures of
children now gone or dead, and of his wife, austere and
thin.

The old man said, "Why, sir, my wife was a saint.
When she had her first baby she didn't know what was
ailin' her till the fourth month. I was ashamed. I had to
up and tell her she was goin' to have a youngun. I felt like
a goat. She was a saint if ever there was one."

Lars laughed and said, "I got to be going up the river
and get my old man out of jail."

"I'd like to go with you," the bartender said. "I
know a man in Hastings who could fix it up. But there's
nobody to keep store. Should I shut up?"

"No," Lars said, "you shouldn't, what with hard
times. Nobody can tell how many pike fishers might be in
for beer between now and sundown, and want to fill up

and maybe want some hard liquor." Lars winked.

And the old man said, "I'd like a snort of hard liquor myself."

Lars said, "Sure, I would too. Why didn't you come out with it sooner?" He took a snort and bought a pint bottle for himself and put it in his pocket. Then he got into his car, the old man, like a broken stick, telling him where the turn was at the brick house.

"My own grandfather laid the bricks in that house and in all the viaducts around about, one of the best masons in the country. He laid every stone and brick worth layin' and was a boozer from way back, drank hard liquor like a baby drinks milk, and lived to a hearty old age, sound as a nut."

"Yes, sir," Lars said, and drove off toward Hastings, now only a few miles away. And he turned at the brick house and came to the corkscrew bridge which he hadn't seen since he was a young man and came here for his marriage license. That's why he knew where the courthouse was, which he entered and went down to the left wing.

The jailer opened the door, grinning, and brought the old man out grumbling. "Well, you took your time about it," in Swedish, and hooked his bones onto the side of the chair, folding his old bent legs under him, then said in broken English, "I told the old woman to send for you. You got to go to Thief River and get my harvest money out of the seaman's chest in the barn, and get me out."

"Why don't she do it?" Lars said.

"She don't know where it is," the old man said cunningly, "and I won't tell her. She might spend it."

Lars laughed. "I got other things to do myself," he said.

The old man said, "You get the money and get me out. It's a hundred and ten dollars."

"A hundred and ten dollars!" Lars whistled. "That's plenty. How much did you make on your wheat?"

"A hundred and twenty. I spent ten already."

"All your harvest money," Lars said.

The old man bent his head but looked from under his shaggy brows with one cunning eye. Lars had to laugh.

"Take a snifter," he said, offering his bottle of moon.

The old man threw back his turkey-gobbler throat, and it turned red slowly from the powerful drink. He took out a half pint from his own lean pocket and filled it from

Lars' bottle, quick as a wink. Lars began to laugh. There they were, sitting in the Hastings jail, as naked of worries as jays. By heavens, he hoped he lived as long as the old man, he hoped he lived forever.

Outside the barred windows he saw the tall black trees standing in the golden day. A fiery juice of life seemed to pour through his huge and powerful frame, and he felt as if he could bend the bars back and he and the old man could climb, like youngsters, through the window and tear across the courthouse lawn, escaping down to the river where they would build a raft and float down to Natchez in the moonlight.

He became excited as if he were going to do all that, and yet he knew that he wasn't going to move. He didn't want to move, sitting on the stool opposite the crafty old man who must still feel the wild burgeoning of the young liquor in his veins; must still feel it though he must be eighty-five if he was a day. Lars suddenly loved the old man. He put his arms around him.

"Don't take any wooden nickels. I'll get the money back. I'll see if I can talk to the sheriff." He wanted to appear young and important to the old man, as if he still had some power in the world because of his physical strength, his vitality.

"Good . . . good boy," the old codger said. "Good boy." And Lars resented it.

"I'll mail the money in tomorrow, I can't waste another day," Lars said at the open door as if he moved, enormously busy, in the processes of a swarming life already ghostly to the old man. But, looking back, he didn't want to leave the old man. There he stood, fragile as a cricket, his hands almost to his swollen knees, so little Lars could have picked up the strong stubborn bones and taken them with him.

The sheriff said, "But he does this every spring and fall. He's a menace — tearing down the highway."

"Did he ever kill anybody? You never heard of him having an accident, did you?"

"No," the sheriff said, taking a drink from Lars' bottle, "but that's because we always catch him in time. Danged if I ever see the beat of it."

They both grinned. "Aw, cripes," Lars said, "a man's got to have his fling; you know hot it is." They both grinned and sat a while. "Have another drink," Lars said.

"Don't care if I do. Well, it's a pretty stiff fine, all right, but them fly cops . . ."

"The old man's pretty canny when he's drunk; just as a grasshopper spitting juice, he's harmless. You and I are getting on a little, Sheriff."

"Speak for yourself, Lars; I'm as chipper as I was at fifty."

"Why, Sheriff, a man wouldn't take you for a day over fifty."

"And you, Lars Larson . . . it's amazing. They must take good care of you 'cross the river there. What keeps you so young?"

"Aw, you're full of taffy."

"Well, you get me fifty and I'll just have to have another snifter."

When Lars left he looked up at the barred window. Even if the old man was looking out he knew there would be no sign of it. He would simply look out at his son and the strong blood feeling would be tender between them, strong as the sweet day. He stood in the strong light feeling that tumult in his blood caused by seeing the old man, feeling his blood kin rousing him to this wild warmth. He stood under a tree and took a swig from his bottle.

He drove back swiftly; it was getting coolish. Once he stopped and tore the melons open with his hands and ate them, and they went good with the hot corn liquor burning in him. Driving through the hills, he passed the tavern of the old man and the dog, drove into the hills where the valleys were cool and dark and the hill tips rose, catching the sunlight. Letting the old car rattle down a hill he saw a marvelous orchardful of crab apples, and his mouth watered. By Jesus, he hadn't seen such a fine orchard of crab apples in many moons, the trees were loaded, they shone red and smart.

Without even thinking, now that the liquor was warm and strong in him, he turned in, drove up a turning road to a ramshackle house in the curve, and stopped the car. It was very still. Some ducks walked across to the water trough. It didn't seem as though anybody was home. He sat there in a little doze, guessing maybe he had drunk too much, and now his bones would ache, but he didn't feel any ache yet, only pleasantness. He could hear a bull kicking the sides of the barn, a steady thud. He dozed off, seeing everything through his half-closed eyelids. It all looked warm as if swimming in a golden syrup, and he heard a woman's voice from the house say:

"Do you want something?" He opened his eyes, and saw a woman in the door, her arm lifted so he could almost see the pit. She was shading her eyes, looking at him.

He moved his limbs; they felt heavy and fine. "Yes, ma'am," he said, feeling easy and hearty. He got out of the car. "That's a fine orchard of crab apples you got here," he said, going up to her, and she put down her arm and smiled easily.

"Yes," she said, "the best in these parts, if I do say it."

"Yes, sir," he said, "it's hard to get a crop like that what with pests and drouth, and tarnation in general."

She laughed, still standing in the door. He saw what fine arms she had, burned, and he could see the strong muscle turning on the bone, yet the flesh was ripe and full.

"How's chances for getting a peck of them apples?" he said, easy and slow, looking at her. She looked right back at him.

"All right," she said: "we ain't got any in the house, though. We ain't chucked 'em down yet. We'll have to go out and pick them up."

"Fine!" he said. "That suits me. I haven't been turned loose in such an orchard since I was knee-high to a grasshopper."

"Well, all right," her heavy slumberous voice said. "Wait and I'll get a basket."

He stood at the door rubbing his hands together. He felt heavy and fine. He wondered if she could tell he'd been drinking. Shucks, he hadn't been drinking much — just enough to put silk on his bones.

She came out with a bonnet on that hid her hair and face and made her body more noticeable. He walked beside her to the orchard and he could feel the strong easy swing of her legs, and her body settling down easy on each step, then rising and settling again. By God, he liked that — the way she walked. Her strong breasts hung down in her wrapper and she walked swiftly, stooping to pick up the apples in her brown talons. He picked up apples too, dropping them into the basket. On one side the apple was warm, on the ground side cool as a cucumber.

His mouth watered from touching them and he set his teeth into one, and the white crab juice sprang out on his mouth and chin, and ran into his fingers. It was a fine taste, and he looked at the woman while he was eating, and she went on swiftly scooping up the apples which she was

now putting into her apron and dropping into the basket
all at once. He felt like a slacker in the face of her swift
voluptuous industry, and he spit out the core and began to
pick again. He found himself picking close to her and he
felt heady. The orchard was silent around them, and as far
as he could tell, all the menfolks must be out in the fields or
gone to town with hogs or steers. Apples dropped from the
trees around them, or farther away in the orchard, and a
strange communication was between them as they walked
under the little gnarled apple trees of the orchard.

And he only half heard when she said, "I think there
was a wind last night. I think enough have shaken on the
ground."

He was walking powerfully beside her and he felt
again that strong and terrible desire. It was mixed with the
feeling of the whole day, some last redolence of the blood
before winter. He felt a fright to think of his towering
strength diminishing in him in ills, aches, and debility,
until one morning in some fall he would be old and dying
and could feel no more the plow, the hot resurgence of
spring and brandy, the potent flood of desire and life.

They passed through a grove of live oaks, and hanging
from the trees by their feet were two steers, freshly but-
chered, their entrails a-light in the sun, blood soaking into
the ground.

"Sure," he heard himself saying, "a right smart wind
down the valley." But all the time he felt the strong
shifting of her weight in a thrust of energy, and the
down-dropping relaxation of her whole body as she settled
on the earth, and he saw the long sweep of her hips as her
dress fell in front and slightly hitched in back.

She said, "My husband took the steers to market,"
and it startled him.

They were alone there then, and he felt the subtle and
curious surge of her strong bending hips, the rhythmic dip
toward the earth and then the slight rise as she dropped the
apples in her apron, which she held up with her other hand.
Then she lifted her head in the hot silence and he saw her
young and burned face from within the sunbonnet, and
most of all he saw her eyes looking at him as if he were a
young man in his prime, and her woman's mouth slightly
open and the moisture of her movement shining on her
face. And then she lowered her head again and filled the
basket.

He didn't move. It was very quiet with just the apples dropping. It was the moment. He knew that. The baskets were full, the sun was setting. He moved towards her and he felt her stiffen and wait. And he stood very close to her and as he reached for the basket he touched the golden down on her arms and he saw the turn of the young powerful flesh up the bone gleaming and sweating. His big brown hand tightened around the belly of her arm and she did not move. He felt her breath, odorous of apples, and the sun hot on one cheek.

Then he took the basket from her, and he knew the moment was over forever and he felt a kind of huge peace with the slanting sun. And he walked silently beside her, and it was as if she felt it too. He poured the two baskets of apples into the back seat and saw it was nearly full of the little apples, cheek by jowl. He ate another, fingering the round tiny cheek.

He turned to the woman, who stood by the well, her face half hidden and secret. He started to say, "How much?" But something in her forbade him, as she stood there, still accessible to him. And he knew he would always see her standing there in the long fingers of the sun, like the opulent earth, like the great harvest, like all of his life, open-handed, generous, sweet-smelling.

"I thank you," he said, taking off his hat and dropping it. "I surely do thank you." He felt his face reddening as he stooped to pick up his hat. And he still felt her generous silence as he started the car and called good-bye. And when he looked back at the turn of the road she was gone.

The dusk caught him before he crossed the bridge towards home. The village looked strange and neat to him, and he drove into his own yard with relief as if he had had a great adventure, gone through dangers. The lamp was lit in the kitchen and the girls' faces clustered in the door. He shouted at them, and went through, the warm hands touching him, and the bodies of the girls changing into women, and their bright tender faces towards him.

His wife stood at the stove. She turned her startled face towards him, not knowing what he felt, nettled by his absence. Supper was all ready and he washed his hands and sat down, and took a fresh piece of bread. They had baked that day, and he could see his wife at the stove looking askance, not knowing what had befallen him.

The girls at the table in the lamplight were full of questions, and he began to swing into his story, making it a fine one. He felt strange and looked at the faces around him, and they seemed almost comic. It was like some Swedish fairy tale where you leave a picnic, go around a mountain, meet a gnome, marry, live a whole life, and then come back and your mortal wife is just wiping up the dishes from the meal not half an hour ago.

His wife was frying potato pancakes; so she stood in the half dark at the stove, and he knew she was looking at him and hanging on every word he was speaking to them. Once he stopped and lifted his head. "Bet you don't believe that, Mama, eh?"

She snorted in the dark. "Bet you got drunk yourself," she said, "bet you had a girl with you."

The girls made little screams and clucks. He threw back his head and laughed and the girls laughed with him. "What do I need of a girl?" he said, looking around at the strong, gleaming daughters' flesh. "What do I need of any more girls?" And they smiled and were pleased.

He felt strong and fine. His wife sniffed at the stove, and he got up, pretending to get water, and he stopped on the dark side away from the lamp, beside her. And she kept on turning the pancakes cooking on top of the stove. The fire from the cracked iron flew over her face, and he could smell the good smell of her flesh and of her hands. He put his hand on her thigh where the children could not see, and put his wind-burned face into her warm neck.

She turned her head, laughing into her shoulder. "Lars," she said, "the children, please —" And her face was full of fright and desire and embarrassment. "Please, Lars . . ."

And from the darkness of his fields came the full rich lowing of cows.

To Hell with You, Mr. Blue!

He said, "It's much better to go on the bus. It will be over in no time." He and Ona were sitting in the bus station waiting for the bus to Madison, because it was better not to have any children now because — how could they follow the races then, and what about Florida in the winter?

"Dizzy Dean sure gave them a wallop," he said, turning the sports page.

"Yeah," she said, her hands tight around the new bag he bought her from cleaning up on the Cardinals.

"All right, Hon, here we are," he said, leaning down for her suitcase, his jowls lean over his strong teeth, his nervous hands still gripping the paper where it told about Dizzy Dean and how Ohio had just come through.

The bus pulled smooth and huge against the curb. "Boy, she's a beauty," he said; "look at that — streamlined — ain't that a beauty, Hon?"

"Yeah," she said.

"It will be over in no time," he said, patting her arm. "Goodbye, Hon. Send me a telegram from Madison, will you? Goodbye, baby."

"I suppose anyway it would look like you and be a ball player."

"Jesus," he said. "So long. I won't wait. I've got to see a fellow."

She saw him going lean and lone down the street, and hate gorged in her mouth like vomit.

She didn't know when the bus pulled out. For hours they kept plunging into the country and she lay back, sick. When I come back, she thought, I'll be divided. I'll be empty. It's smart to be empty. I'll be empty and wise. The mist lay over the dark plowed crevasse of the spring earth.

She felt him instantly, opened her eyes, saw him standing in the aisle, sharp and neat, changing his hat for a cap, folding up his flowered scarf like a woman, pulling his coattails apart to sit between them for neatness' sake. He was neat as a trigger. Her senses sharpened in alarm. A certain kind of moth comes out after night, with so powerful an odor, both repulsive and attractive, and actually seems to permeate your flesh, so if you raise your

arms or smell your own hands you would think the moth
had darkened your skin.

She looked through the glass at the swelling, chording
earth. She put her hands against the cold glass, against the
steel skeleton. She moved as far as she could against the
window away from him. They began going through a fog
that came in wisps at first in the groins of the hills and then
thickened like whey.

The bus kept going swiftly through Wisconsin. Wisconsin has a powerful beauty. The girls were chattering,
bold slender girls, excited by voyaging with strange men.
They seemed nervous and precocious, fabulously slender.
The man who sat beside her kept looking at the girls with a
little sneer around his mouth. He made her feel ponderous
and heavy. Women are not his gamble, she thought, oh,
no, he would hardly take a chance on that. Instantly she
knew he was a gambler. He seemed to be striking against
her making her feel as clear as a bell.

The big lanky boys started sparking the girls. They
seemed enormous, gay and dapper, but with such a physical emptiness they were like sounding brass to her. They
passed through towns, past the first national bank, library,
newspapers, picture show, and bon ton beauty parlors.

Finally he bent a little towards her, coughed into a silk
handkerchief, and said in a delicate high voice, "Look,
what time will we be in Madison?"

"I don't know, I'm sure," she said, coldly.

He looked with his down-slanting eyes at the back of
the seat in front, and she saw his nervous slender hands
with the thumbs turned back, hanging like delicate boughs
from his wrists, a little heavy. "My name is Blue," he said
to the back of the seat. "My family used to call it Bleu, but
now it is just plain Blue, that's what it is now."

She suddenly had to laugh, he looked so like a little
plucked cock. He had had sometimes a peculiar little
electric manhood in him, but now he looked exactly like a
little plucked cock.

"Blue," she said, pursing her lips to keep from a wild
snort of laughter.

"Just plain Blue," he said forlornly.

What had got him down so low? She said, "Are you
French?"

He looked at her suddenly in pure astonishment, and
the black hair going down his slim head seemed to stand on

end a little, exactly like a cockscomb. "Why, no one ever asked me that in America," he said. "No one ever thought anything about it," he said in utter astonishment, as if he had been going softly in the underbrush of America, hardly seen, laying his bets.

"You're a gambler," she said.

Now his cockscomb did bristle and rise right up on his tiny cranium. "How did you know?"

"Well," she said, "I thought you might be half Indian and half French."

"Oh, no." Now he was excited. "Oh, but no, *full* French."

"O.K.," she said, "full French. O.K. with me."

He leaned toward her. "How did you know I was a gambler?"

She lowered her eyes to his quick hands that turned over in the light like something turning out of the dark underroot, and the strong turned-back thumb and the whiteness as if they slept in the day and at night the tips knew the Jack, the Queen and the Ten. She couldn't look above his hands — she felt something dreadful would happen if she looked him square in the eye, she didn't know what. He turned toward her that soft curiously probing nervous energy. She knew he had huge dark eyes, very round and wide, wide open and dark and blank, his energy being in his nerves, in the nerves of the hand where you could see the thick gorged arteries that fattened on the lean backs.

"I am all French," he said, "I have crossed the ocean fourteen times, that is a lot, yes?"

"Oh, yes," she said, "a lot."

"Oh, it is wonderful, wonderful," he said in his peculiar alone little ecstasy. "Have you crossed the ocean?"

"Oh, certainly," she lied, "I have crossed the ocean." He would look down on her if she had not crossed the ocean.

"I went to Catholic school," he said sadly. Oh, he was sad, it came out of him like some dusk emitted from his pores. "My folks live here now."

They went plunging through the thicketed hills, now darkening in the dusk.

Suddenly he seemed to excite himself on his own whetstone. "Listen," he said, "I've had it easy, very very easy, very very very easy. I've had plenty of dough."

"Fine," she said.

"Oh, but it is sad now," he said quickly, ducking down, just collapsing beside her. "Listen," he said, "You wouldn't believe it. I could sit here and tell you about my life. I've been sitting very very pretty. I'm sitting very very pretty right now. Would you believe it?"

"Oh, yes," she said, turning her mouth down bitterly, "I would believe it."

"I don't know what it is," he said, "the bottom has dropped out of everything."

"Everything?" she mocked.

"Oh, everything. Look, here I am going around piddling around like this, making long jumps in the dark and what for?"

"I couldn't say," she said.

"To lay a bet on a horse. I have to monkey around like this because the law says you can't lay only so much in one spot. Piddling, a little dab at a time. Can you believe it?"

"Oh, I can believe it," she said, and she saw he had big circles around his great blank frightened eyes.

"Fighting, gambling, everything, what is it now?"

"Well, what is it? She thought she was going to vomit. She could wear him and she could wear her husband for a pin, or crush their tiny excited bones in her hands.

God damn men who are gamblers, baseball players, prize fighters, horse racers, driving a woman batty.

They whizzed through the villages at evening time. The houses began to be lighted, colts followed mares into the barns, children burned with the first sun were adrowse from heat. The bus stopped in little towns you could never see again. Two young girls came around the corner of a bank swishing and chattering. I was like them, Ona thought, now I am different. They were turning their mascaraed eyes towards trouble, trouble heavying on their bodies. I won't have to see it, she thought, I'll be gone. I don't have to see it, but you know it is coming like a cyclone. The bus leaves in five minutes.

They passed a woman driving two horses with tails magnificently braided and mud hanging from their winter furred bellies. She thought she would never forget that woman, as for an instant she looked into her wide hanging breast and at the child only half broken from her, still moulded to her thighs. There she sat holding the reins of the horses so they would not bolt, poised in the midst of her strong life, in birth, crops, baking of bread. Mr. Blue did not see her. He was silently sleeping, his head hanging off his thin neck a little.

She had to look at him when he wasn't looking. At his narrow shoulders, at his tiny pointed ears, and the black hairs growing on his green white skin. She had to look at him and she felt he was half awake like a cat. She felt heavy and beautiful beside his quickness.

The sun had long gone. They changed drivers, this time a stout strong fellow, very safe. The mist rose from the river and began to cover the earth. Mr. Blue sat up and looked into the milky dark. "Where are we?" he said.

"I don't know." She felt contempt for his little fright and anxiety.

"Now, if it weren't for this law," he said sadly, "I wouldn't have to be riding like this to Madison. I have to go to Madison now to place another bet. Oh, it's piddling."

"I have to go to Madison," she said, "I don't like it either."

"Yes, gambling isn't what it used to be."

"No," she said, "it isn't."

"I've certainly had it easy in my time," he said, spreading out his hands. "I've had plenty, plenty of what it takes. Say, why don't you become a booker in Chicago? Most of the bookers are women now. It's awful."

"I can imagine," she said.

"You can't go anywhere without stumbling over women now. They get in your hair. Women are everywhere, drinking, making the love, at the races. It used to be you knew when a woman would turn up. Now they're everywhere, throwing up along the curb, everywhere. Phew!"

"Yes," she said, seeing his huge distaste. She felt a huge laughter in her. I hope they overrun your nice neat little gambling world. I hope they spoil everything.

"Women are fixed, too," Mr. Blue said.

"Fixed?" Her blood ran cold. "Fixed?"

"Sure. They just want it and what they can get. They're all fixed."

"So, women are fixed."

"Oh, but certainly."

"They're all fixed?"

"Everything is fixed," Mr. Blue said.

Oh, you could wear him on your wrist with a chiffon handkerchief, or like a lizard on your neckpiece.

The fog kept getting thicker. They only rose out of it on the hills where the moon rode the sky. Mr. Blue talked more in the dark. The lights were out and the driver had to go very slowly. They would be in Madison at twelve according to schedule, but they were running behind. They would be late. She put her hand under her coat lightly. I hope we never get there. I hope we never get anywhere.

"So you're awfully smart, Mr. Blue," she said bitterly.

"Oh, I know the world from A to Z."

From a tomb, you mean."

"Oh, not bad, but I know it. I've been around. Oh, I've cracked that oyster O.K."

She had to look at his slender cocky head, the pale neck where the hair had been clipped, the odor of Sen-Sen and eau de cologne, the narrow faun's shoulders, the curious nervous body. Like her husband's. On the trigger excitement. You could crack his little head like a fine nut between your hands.

"I've been around. I've seen things, lady. I've seen 'em come and go. I've been in some pretty important places."

"Have you, really?"

"Oh, certainly. I'm not a ham. I'm going around now on this piddling business, but I'm no ham. I been in the big time. Don't you believe it?"

"Oh, sure, certainly, I believe anything you say."

"Fine. Well, it's the truth, I wouldn't fool you. Why, I was press agent once for Dempsey. The great Dempsey — you know, the great great boxer."

"Oh, sure, certainly, I know. So you knew Dempsey."

"Did I know him! We were just like that. Oh, a king, a prince, a man among men. I was with him. I came right out of the ring with him after that pretty knockout. Oh, that was sweet, the sweetest thing I ever saw. Oh, that night I'll never forget. That was the greatest night of my life. Oh, that was sweet, as sweet a one as I've ever seen. It's worth living to see that come over, swift and sweet."

He wasn't describing love. "Did you know his wife?" she said.

"Sure, of course, natural. I knew his wife."

"What's the matter? You look like you tasted something bad."

"It's bad for a great champ like that to get himself hooked up. A bird like that should never get himself married, that's what I say."

"That's what you say."

"Sure, I say it and I mean it. A bird like that shouldn't do it. It's a crime."

"Sure," she said, "a crime."

"Sure, a crime. What business is it of a fellow like that hooking up? Oh, that night I'll never forget it. Why should he get spliced after a thing like that?"

"I don't know, I'm sure," she said. She felt pretty bitter against him. "She's a nice person," she said feebly.

"Oh, sure, she's all right, but he's got no business. Why, a fellow like that is sitting on top of the world. He can have everything. I was with them after that and he could have everything. But prize fighting is different now."

"Is it fixed, too?"

"Oh sure, is it? Is it ever fixed! Look, wrestling is fixed, too."

"Is it possible? Women, now wrestling."

"Wrestling worst of all."

"Is it possible? You've cracked that nut, too?"

"Sure," he said, "I know that game, too." He grinned. "From A to B, too. Look, wrestling is fixed, stands to reason. Want me to tell it?"

"Sure," she said, "I'll keep it a secret."

"Now look, you could break a fellow's foot, couldn't you? It stands to reason. If it weren't fixed, why don't they break each other's bones? You never hear of it, do you? Why don't they if it ain't fixed?"

"I like to see it," she said, "better than hitting."

"Oh, sure," he said, "a woman's soft like that. But it's fixed. There's nothing as good as boxing. Oh, man, the sweet fights I've seen. But boxing is fixed, too. I don't hardly never go to a match any more. Minneapolis is nuts about boxing. I never go, though, since Dempsey is out of the ring. Boxing ain't the same since he's gone. The Champ . . ." He turned his blind ecstatic face towards her. "The greatest living champ . . . he was the greatest that ever lived . . ."

Love, O manlove in his voice. "So boxing is fixed, too," she said.

"Sure, boxing is fixed, too."

"I hope it's all fixed, Mr. Blue," she said.

The bus driver got pretty nervous. The mist rose heavy now and the encircled moon rode high amidst the thick thrusts of spectral trees and the fog flowed past the windows like milk. Suddenly they would rise directly out of it into a terrifying clarity that made them feel the cliff was striking them, that the moon moved into their faces.

Everybody got kind of nervous. The girls were half asleep lying against the shoulders of the young men. Mr. Blue got very nervous and wriggled in his seat, and tried to look out to see where the driver was going. The road was muddy, and they went very slowly; the driver had to open the door sometimes to get a line on the shoulder of the muddy road. When they struck an easy stretch Mr. Blue tried to sleep leaning forward, sharp as a needle, his head on his folded wrists; but she knew he would be half awake to see what would be happening, how the wheel would turn. He slept like a cat ready to spring into a nervous spasm, or snarl in a delicate sneer.

It was really pitch dark out. You couldn't see a thing. The bus heaved them all forward and stopped. The driver wiped the sweat off his head and swore. "When we get to Madison," he said, "I'm going to jump in the air and click my heels together."

Sure enough, Mr. Blue sprang alive laughing. "I would like to see that, too," he said, chuckling soundlessly. An old man was standing bending his head against the roof, peering out. You couldn't see a thing. It was just like thick cream out. He was a serious grizzled old man bending over looking at the fog. He said, "Let me out." Mr. Blue said, "He's yellow. He wants to get out." Everybody heehawed. The half sleeping boys seemed to have gigantic faces with huge ear handles that they turned toward Mr. Blue. The driver opened the bus door letting the fog curl in like spilled milk. The old man stepped out and was whirled away as if he had never been. "Good-night," he said on the wind and the driver mopped his head. "Good-night," he said to nobody.

"For Christ's sake," said Mr. Blue shuddering, "I didn't have to come on this bus. I can afford anything. I got money in my pockets and I come on this lousy bus."

Ona felt such a loathing for him. She could twist him in her hands until his eyes sprang out. "So everything is fixed," she said. The wheels spun in the mud. When the mist lifted it showed the soft dangerous shoulder, exposing their danger and frightening them.

"Look, why do I have to travel around in this lousy bus risking my life just to place a little measly bet?"

"What a tragedy," she said clinging to the seat, "a major tragedy."

"I'll say it is. Everything is fixed. Not what it used to be by a long shot."

Sad, oh sad.

He clung to the seat, his eyes popped out in terror, and he tried to peer from side to side into nothing. They struck a little stretch of half good road and breathed easier. "I used to enjoy," Mr. Blue said, his teeth chattering, "God Christ, I used to enjoy. Do you know I was with Wrigley's ball team? I used to go to Catalina and see them wind up every spring . . . I was keen for baseball, never missed a game, traveled clean across the country to see St. Louis play. And do you know I was right there in St. Louis the other day, had tickets for the game, and do you know?"

"What?" The bus shivered and threw them all over so she had to cling to the sill of the window.

"Oh, terrible," Mr. Blue chattered. "Why do we stand it? Can you believe it. I was right there on the spot and wanted to see Dizzy wallop 'em across and do you know I never went near the ball park? Can you believe it?"

"Impossible."

"Can you believe it?"

"I can believe it. I *must* believe it."

"I don't know what's got into me." The driver let the bus drop into a hole and spun the wheels and roared the engine and lifted heavily out. "I didn't have to come on this lousy bus and now look, we'll all be killed. I've got my pockets chuck full of dough and I buy a ticket on this bus."

She laughed silently and held to the window to keep from lurching against him. Come on, little man, don't get excited, take a little gamble on your white bones, shoot your own bones for a crap game once, darling, take a chance on your own dancing bones and you won't look so under a plank.

"Listen," Mr. Blue said, "do you think I am going to be sick? I'm getting seasick." He held his handkerchief to his mouth. "Listen, girlie, you come to Chi and get a job

in the booking office, lay your money right and inside of
a year you'll be rich, lay your money with the smart
guy . . ."

"I don't care for it."

"What?"

"I don't like it."

"You'll make a lot of dough."

"I don't care for it. I don't want a lot of dough."

"Jesus, I do. I want a lot of money. I spend a lot of
money. I need a lot of money. I can't stop needing it or
spending it. I need it and I spend it. I don't have to ride in
this lousy bus going through a fog like this."

The thick rich milk flowed around them. Miserably
Mr. Blue rocked with the bus, his handkerchief to his
mouth. "Jesus," he said, "so you don't want money. I
can remember a long time ago when I felt like that. I
wanted something . . . I felt that a long time ago. I can just
remember it, imagine that, I can just remember . . ."

"I can imagine it."

"But, Christ, I need money now. I need things. See
this suit? This is a hundred dollar suit . . ."

"Is it possible!"

"Yeah, feel that, that goods there, just put that between your fingers . . ."

"I wouldn't feel it for a million bucks." She wouldn't
touch him with a ten foot pole. The bus heaved them all
forward and the wheels spun as it hung in mid-air.

"For Christ's sake," said Mr. Blue, shivering in such
utter sensibility and terror. The wheels spun, the engine
roared, the bus groaned, pulled out and ground along the
mud. "I can afford anything, can you believe it. I didn't
have to come on this bus and I have come on it."

"I can believe it," Ona said. "Certainly, why make
such a fuss? This is alright. You're a poor gambler, really.
Do you just gamble with money? My husband, too. A
diamond is an awful little spot to gamble your life on.
What if Ohio did come through . . ."

"Don't get mad," he cried, cringing, lurching
forward into his handkerchief and retching.

She felt like a roaring bulwark of flesh beside him, a
tidal wave of woman's flesh, terrible in wrath.

"Why do we stand it?" cried Mr. Blue in misery, and
he leaned his black fox terrier head on his white hands.

And she had to look at him as if his little black
cranium bore her some secret, his tiny pointed ears, the

black hair growing like bracken out of his white rock
wrists. I know you, Mr. Blue. My husband, too. You
don't care for anything that doesn't touch you on the nerve
ends like horse racing, like seeing a horse you've bet on
come down the course, like seeing the cards lie right, like
seeing Dempsey move in with a neat haymaker. What
chance has a woman got with this? If the cards lie right,
what price a woman? — if the horse flesh comes in pretty
and neat, what's the use of a woman? You can feel that in
every bit of your delicate nervous twitching skin, Mr. Blue.
You can't depend upon ball players, card, dice, horse
players or prize fighters to make fat children drop down in
season. A soft luminous volume seemed to fill her body
like love for this earth.

In one hour they would be in Madison now. She
began to make a telegram letting the words form in front
of her. She felt large, delicious, wonderful and terrible.

She started and saw Mr. Blue looking at her with one
eye, like an animal in a thicket. Her blood shot and
cascaded down her in a terrible black fury as if splitting her
veins and thrumming against her skin.

"I was watching you," said Mr. Blue. "I'm afraid of
you."

"Yes," she said. She knew clearly the words of the
telegram. They came out of the fog, lifted into the hills
where little firs grew.

Mr. Blue's face drifted down sharp in the moonlight.
"What do you enjoy?" he said.

She couldn't cry out to him she enjoyed her husband,
gambling blood and bones then. She felt terrible and wonderful.

"Oh, I used to enjoy," said Mr. Blue, continually
wiping his mouth with his handkerchief. "God Christ, I
used to enjoy. Do you know what I enjoy now?"

"I couldn't say." The bus ran along now swift and
smooth.

"There is only one thing I enjoy now. Everything else
is fixed, could you believe it?"

"I could believe it. Shoot."

"I enjoy food."

"Food?"

"Food."

"Well," she burst out laughing, "for Christ's sake!"

"I walk blocks," he says, "blocks and blocks to get
something to eat, something very nice to eat."

"What, for instance?"

"Oh, something very, very nice."

"Like what?"

"Oh, I don't know, something nice, prepared nice, you know, tasty, seasoned up good. But this is hard to find. I have even gone to another town to get something better to eat."

"Is it possible?" she cried.

"And I gamble on it. I toss up a coin."

"With yourself?" she cried out, and the moon rode wildly through the pine. "With only yourself?"

"Yes," he said, "I make a bet with myself whether they will be having steak and mushrooms on Thursday night or on Sunday night. Sometime I gamble whether going to another town I can get maybe crepe suzettes . . ."

Oh, Mr. Blue, how desolate . . . how desolate.

"Madison," the bus driver said.

She pushed out of the bus. Mr. Blue cried, "Wait!"

She ran up the long steps to the telegraph station. She wrote as quick as she could: "To hell with you and Mr. Blue. I am going to have it."

We'll Make Your Bed

We were down in the hollow. It was a sunny morning and Slim and me were trying to be quiet so as not to wake Mr. and Mrs. Lamb who were on their honeymoon. We had the frame of the woodsy bed all set up by ten o'clock and Slim kept looking at the modern log cabin of the Lamb's and making remarks that had me bent over with laughing.

Slim was a fast one before the war and it didn't slow him up none, and he was making jokes about old Mr. Lamb the Lumber King taking unto hisself a blushing bride at the age of sixty. No getting around it, Mrs. Lamb was a looker, a nice soft woman. All the things you go through, I'll swan your old lady gets to be like just something around; you like her, she's comfortable as an old shoe when she ain't snapping at you like a bullwhip, but you don't feel it like you did at first and that's a fact.

"I hope mama doesn't come down here with our lunch. I told her we was raising old pines from the river bottom at ninety an hour."

"O Lord," Slim said, "don't worry, she'll be comin' round the mountain whistle time. No woman'd miss lookin' up at the windows of honeymooners even if they's old enough for a wooden kimono. She'll be steamin' down the hill and that's for certain and sure."

My old woman let out one of her tall whoops when I told her the truth at first that Slim and me got a job making all these little doodads for Mrs. Lamb, bird houses like little log cabins, cute as all get out, but as Slim said, "A hell of a piddlin' for two lumberjacks who in their day could blast a river and break up a log jam single-handed." It was bad enough when we had to fix up the old outhouse which was of good mahogany and Mrs. Lamb wanted it oiled up swank and a moon and crescent carved on it, so she and friends on Sunday afternoon took pictures of the thing as if it was a huge joke or something. It beats all when you think my old woman has been after me day and night to get indoor plumbing so the girls could be raised like ladies.

We made a summer house over the river and that was when Mr. Lamb said, "Boys, Mrs. Lamb wants a woodsy bed now." I couldn't stand to tell the old lady and I made up the story about the deadheads. I couldn't stand the gaff at home any longer. My old lady barring none has got probably the longest, loudest, rip-snorting, rib-cracking sneer that they is anywhere on this green earth. It was bad enough when I told them about the woodsy bird houses and the flower bower. My old lady is lean as a whip snake and even if she has had eight kids on our old farm, four dead and four living, she's fast and quick and full of vinegar all right.

"Itty bitty bird houses," yell the kids like a bunch of coyotes. "The champion, the birling champion, the fastest man to twirl a cant-hook, works up to making itsy bitsy beds for Honey" — this being what Mr. Lamb calls his new bride. "Honey," says my wife, and the tone of it would make a hole in a pine log, "Honey," she says, "Oh! I want to bake my bread outdoors in an oven — oh, it is so picturesque — it is so woodsy —" And Elmer, the spitting image of his ma, begins to priss around saying in the high voice of Mrs. Lamb, "Oh, make me a little woodsy house hanging over the river. Mr. Lamb being an old lumber maggot and all. . . ." And the other kids, like magpies getting in line, begin to jibber — "Lumber maggot . . . lumber maggot."

"Good for you," says my old lady, bitter as lye. "So after workin' your heart out forty years or maybe more in these woods, you work up to hunting little saplings for a woman that never bore a chick nor child. . . ."

I looked into my stew ashamed. "Well," I says, "this is hard times — hard to get work — a man ought to be glad. . . ."

"Glad," she explodes like stump dynamite, "glad!" And I don't want to look at her for a fact. I went out by the river and thought of the fine masts, growing straight into the sky, I helped in my time snake down to the river, down to the sea. The finest spars and masts that ever went to sea we tooken right out of here. It was a fine country then, with horse racing every Saturday at Stillwater.

"I ain't never stayed in bed this long in the morning, even the first night me and Anna was married," Slim said, looking at the honeymooners' windows.

"I guess a honeymoon is a honeymoon no matter what age you're at."

We had set our sawhorses up far enough away from the window so as not to disturb them none. We had got pretty beech saplings from the woods. Slim and me, I guess, know every kind of wood there is being and growing in these woods. I remember some trees like they was people.

"When they get up," I said, "they're comin' out here and give us some good advice."

"The bastards," Slim said, "they better not come out here tellin' *me* anything about what to do with wood. They better not tell me how to make a bed."

"A woodsy bed," I said and he said with a snort, "Yeah, a blankety-blank woodsy bed." Slim has got quite a store of honeymoon jokes of one shade and another and him telling them all morning, while we was cutting the saplings for the posts, kind of got my dander up.

Then I saw her, dangerous and fiery like a flag on a battleship, coming down the hill with our lunch, tough and wiry, my old woman.

"Jiggers," Slim said, "there's the battle cry. Too late. . . . Prepare to meet thy God."

We pretended to be mighty busy and she bore down on us like a river full of logs let loose by thaw. I never was more scared. She just said, "Well!" and stood there like a little snake looking dangerous out of the brush. "Well," she said again and I had rather a fine bullwhip had curled lovingly around my middle. Slim was grinning, kind of sick-like, and pretending to measure the saplings carefully. "What now?"

I heard my voice break like a young fellow's and I thought the blood would burst my ears. "A bed," I said, hearing my voice squeak. She seemed to jump toward me. "A bed," she hissed.

"A woodsy bed," Slim said, and began to imitate Mr. Lamb, stroking a belly Slim didn't have since he got back from the war. "Honey wants a bed. She's got a dozen beds, some with silk, some with satin, but she's romantic so to speak — yes, Honey is romantic and she says being as how I'm a big lumber man — oh a big lumber man —" and here Slim batted his eyes in an awful way, winking and looking mighty fast and frisky and giving more meaning to it than the words seemed to, "yes, a big lumber man and well Honey it looks like she wants a kind of woodsy bed. . . ."

This even knocked the wind out my old woman and I could see her mouth kind of start to form the words "a woodsy bed." Just then we heard a door slam and voices talking and saw a flash of color and there was Mr. and Mrs. Lamb looking in all the birds' nests to see if they had any birds and it made a kind of tickling fire come in my belly to see them. Mr. Lamb had his arm around her and she was a good full figure of a woman, with something floating around her more like a nightgown than anything else. And before I knew what I was doing I clapped my old woman into the outhouse, told her to be quiet and locked the door from the outside. I was back helping Slim before I started to think and I could see Slim winking at me and we watched them out of the corner of our eyes as they came down the hill from the house looking into all the bird houses, Mrs. Lamb kind of floating in this thingumabob soft and clingy so I couldn't look at her straight. I thought I could see the terrible eye of my old lady looking out the outhouse moon Slim and I had carved.

I began to smell that whiff that comes from Mrs. Lamb when she moves and makes you dizzy. My old lady smells good too in a different way, kind of clean and soapy and of babies. Not a bad smell when you come down to it. But Mrs. Lamb smells like something else, I don't know what, kind of indecent — and seeing them and knowing my old woman is watching and Slim leering and winking at me a kind of flame kept licking up inside me that had some anger in it and something bitter as gall running sap deep, strong and secret.

"They're lookin'," Slim says low, "to see if they've caught any birds in their piddlin' little traps of houses. If I was a bird, I'd fly over and you know what I'd do —"

"Shut up," I says. They are coming down to us holding hands and old man Lamb kind of looking at her with mooning eyes and she's laughing and swinging his hand and stuff floating around her, all filled out a fine figure, and like she never had worn herself to a frazzle like my old lady. They are looking at the stuff that is coming up and she kicks the earth with the toe of her shoe which has a little fluff on it like the stuff around her neck. I know my old lady has got her eye peeled to the crescent moon and will be able to tell the kids all about it come evening.

It's like when they come down to us that we are like the birds or the stuff they have planted, or the woodsy bed, as if they owned us like a dog or a cow, and watching them I knew what my old lady felt. I felt it lick up my insides like a snake tongue.

I got to keep a straight face because I am facing them all the time and it is terrible and comical to see Slim's big eyes turn over in his face as he winks at me and I see in his face too a kind of drawn look as if the fast, hot blood was pouring out of him somewhere. They are coming up slow now. Mr. Lamb says to us, "Hello, boys." A man used to managing has a way of speaking I suppose.

"How are you *Mr.* Lamb," Slim says eyeing down the board he has been planing and I try not to look at Mrs. Lamb because my wife will say I was looking at her all the time.

"Now," says Mr. Lamb, his pudgy hands over his paunch as if he has pride that his woman is a little foolish, "the little woman has changed her mind. She wants the color of the pagoda changed."

"What?" says Mrs. Lamb and I don't know if she is a little deaf or just doesn't listen. Mr. Lamb shouts out what he was telling us. "Oh, but yes," she says, "I don't want it yellow now. I will take all the color off."

"A hell of an idea," says Slim, keeping on with his work. "Should never paint a birch."

"What?" cries Mrs. Lamb, and everything she says she seems to jump and move in the stuff that floats around. "Nothing," Slim says and she begins to watch Slim's hands, tender as a woman's on anything that is made of wood. If Slim was blind as a bat he would still be a good carpenter. He can feel wood in his hands.

"The little woman has changed her mind," Mr. Lamb says, and I can hear my old lady telling the children about it at supper in his very words. "You know how it is with women."

We don't say nothing.

"What?" cries Mrs. Lamb again.

"About the yellow paint," Mr. Lamb says.

"Oh, yes," she says. "What will take it off? I could do it myself."

"Oh, you better let them do it," says Mr. Lamb.

"What about sandpaper?"

Slim spits a gob into the sawdust. "You can't sand-paper a birch. You'll have to get some lye."

"Lye," says Mrs. Lamb.

"Yes, lye," Slim says, taking a good straight look at her. "Something with bite to it."

She looks startled. "Something with bite to it," she says over again looking at Slim.

"Yes," he says impudent-like, I thought, so I got nervous and so did Mr. Lamb. "Yes, with bite in it. . . ."

Slim ignores Mr. Lamb. "Sandpaper won't do it," he says insolent-like, looking right at her as if he looked her up and down.

"Oh, no," says Mr. Lamb nervously, "something with bite to it. You boys get some lye, whatever is needed, at the store, charge it to me, get whatever is needed to fix up the little woman with what she wants."

"Yes, sir," Slim says and Mrs. Lamb seems excited and begins to run around pointing here and there and it must be I imagined it that I could see that black snapping eye looking right out the crescent moon of the outhouse.

"Now," cries Mrs. Lamb, "I just bought two hundred dollars worth of grills and things. I am going to make an outdoor kitchen. They have such wonderful things now for roughing it."

"Two hundred bucks!" I says. I ain't seen a hundred bucks at once since the lumber went out.

"I am going to get back to simple things." She turns and clasps her hands and her fine hair seems to have fallen a little out of a net. "Yes, back to the simple life. That's what we must have."

"The simple life," Slim snorts, and Mr. Lamb gets more nervous.

"Well, how is it going to look, boys? How is it coming?" Mr. Lamb seems forcing himself to be hearty and gay. Slim don't say nothing so I says feeling foolish-like with the eye of my old woman glued on me like a vise, "O.K.," I says, and feel foolish to hear my voice break again in a funny embarrassed way which makes me mad enough to pick up a sapling and lay around me like crazy.

Mrs. Lamb lets out little noises, touching the posts like a ring dove in mating time, fluttering around Slim, who keeps right on planing the board, the shavings falling around. Mr. Lamb says everything twice to Mrs. Lamb, who listens as if she is dreaming and then lets out a little cry as if she is astonished.

"Oh," she jumps and cries around us so you can feel what a fine figure of a woman she is, smiling at you with her painted ripe face. Even from where I am with all the smells of the morning and the fresh smell of the shavings, I can smell her. "Oh, you must have had a hard time finding these wonderful trees for the posts, all four just alike."

Slim doesn't peep so again I says foolishly, "Yes'm."

"They're just beautiful," she lows, "just beautiful." And she comes close to Slim, putting her hand on the saplings, and I can see the back of Slim's neck kind of swell and the back of his ears get red. He moves away, picks up a hammer and makes little nervous jabs like a woodpecker.

"Well," Mrs. Lamb laughs, "I don't understand how you are going to make it. Will you tell poor me about it? Squeezics says I'm the most helpless —"

"That's what she calls me," Mr. Lamb says nervously. I thought Slim was going to laugh right out but he kept on making little taps with his hammer as if everything was falling to pieces.

"Now will that be solid?" Mr. Lamb says, picking up one of the posts. Slim takes the wood away from him. "Solid as a tree," Slim says, and keeps tapping with his hammer. Mr. Lamb picks up another one and feels it with his hands and Slim takes the log away from him and puts it back on the saw buck. "Strong enough," Slim says, looking at Mr. Lamb. A slow, yellow color seems to come . over Mr. Lamb's bald head and then it gets very white.

"It must be strong," Mrs. Lamb says, her eyes wide, looking at Slim.

"Those are A-1 birch saplings," Slim says, taking another one out of Mr. Lamb's paws. "They're strong as God made them and you don't want them any stronger than that."

"Well, it wants to be solid," comes back Mr. Lamb, and his mouth looks grim and he picks up the log from the saw buck.

"It will be all right for you," Slim says.

"I'll tell you how I want it," Mr. Lamb says and Slim takes the marked sapling out of his hand and this time Mr. Lamb doesn't pick it up again.

"I'll tell you how we're makin' it," Slim says. If you know Slim you know this is just before he gets mad and tosses everything out the window. It's a good thing they don't know Slim the way I do. Then he says, "We'll show you how it'll be." So him and me set the bed up. They can see what it will be like and he is holding one side and I am holding the other side, and I don't know what he is up to. His nose is kind of pinched and white. I know this is a bad sign.

There is the framework and we're holding it up and Mr. Lamb looks very wise and says, "Mmmmmm." Mrs.

Lamb looks like she ain't seeing anything but Slim and she
moves closer to him. "Oh, yes," she says and I see her put
her hand on Slim's arm and I see the line in his jaw drawn
tight. He moves away from her, and brazen, she follows
him standing close, and we all look at the damned bed.
"And then" says Slim, biting his words off sharp, "we'll
put her in the river and let her soak. . . ."

"Oh, will you do that?" Mrs. Lamb says, looking
bold at Slim, and I feel ashamed. I just look down at my
hands holding the bed and I feel ashamed, and ashamed
my wife is watching from the outhouse.

"Now I understand it," Mr. Lamb says and Slim
looks at him as if he didn't know how to button up his
pants.

"How will you put it together?" Mrs. Lamb cries and
there is something like the way she smells in her voice.
"This is too, too wonderful. My friends will be crazy
about it. You might get a lot of work." Her eyes are big
and bold on Slim. "You might get a good deal of work
because if this is a success, all my friends might want to
have woodsy beds. Just think of it. . . ."

It was that did it. "I'm making no more woodsy
beds," Slim says. He pulls away from her and the framework falls to the ground.

"How will you put it together so it won't show?" Mr.
Lamb says very important-like as if he knows all about it.

"Screw it," Slim says.

"What?" cries Mrs. Lamb.

"Oh, yes," Slim says as big as life, the white line
showing along his jaw, "we'll have to screw it."

Mr. Lamb comes to and shouts at Mrs. Lamb, "He
says they will have to screw it."

"Oh, yes," Mrs. Lamb says kind of lazy, her eyes
bigger than ever.

"It won't hurt the wood none," Slim says, "won't
hurt a thing."

"Oh, certainly," Mr. Lamb says too loudly.

I feel good for the first time, like a big spurt of laughter and strength came into my stomach.

"Oh, but yes," cries Mrs. Lamb. "How wonderful. I
understand."

"Yes," Slim says and I know now he is going to do
something for sure and certain. 'You better understand."

"Come in, Honey," Mr. Lamb says. "Breakfast I am
sure is ready. All right boys, go ahead. Go right ahead.

Get whatever you want. Charge it to me. You know what to do. I'll leave it to you. Get whatever you want."

Slim stood with his hands clenched big as tree bolls. Mr. and Mrs. Lamb went up to their house and Mrs. Lamb looked back. "The bitch," Slim said, loud. He picked up the framework of the bed and holding it above his head, with the heinie still from the Army, he walked to the edge of the bluff. Quick as a flicker my old woman darted out of the outhouse and she picked up the saplings and I saw her running after him, her body like a bat out of hell, for all the hate and sorrow of her life. And I felt this flick of strength up my neck and love for that strong tough flicker of a woman. I stood beside Slim laughing and throwing the last birch into the river. I am laughing so that Mr. and Mrs. Lamb turned at their house startled and frightened. "Charge it to me. Get whatever you want. You know what to do."

And my old woman began to laugh and she slammed me on the back and I saw her black whippersnapper eyes, looking at me again, in the same harness, the good bit in our mouth, together again. "Oh, an outdoor oven," she cried, flouncing like a witch, and Slim and I looked at her bitter strength like a fine aged wood. "Oh, a woodsy bed," she cried.

I haven't shouted across the river like that for a hell of a time. I opened my mouth and bellowed and it went down deep and came out strong, "We'll make your goddamned bed. . . ."

And it struck the rocks across and echoed back as if we had friends across the river — we'll make your bed — we'll make your bed.

Our laughter echoed back too, striking, emerging in air pockets, on wind currents until all the hills and old trees left rotting on the river bottom took it up, shook it out, beat it up and threw it back.

Published volumes of Meridel Le Sueur's writings, excluding stories for children, include:

Salute to Spring, 1940, 1977 (International, N.Y.). Stories.

North Star Country, 1945 (Duell, Sloan and Pearce, N.Y.) People's history.

Crusaders, 1955 (Blue Heron Press, N.Y.). Biographical.

Corn Village, 1970 (Stanton and Lee, Sauk City, Wisc.). Stories.

Rites of Ancient Ripening, 1975, 1976 (Vanilla Press, Minneapolis). Poems.

Song for My Time, 1977 (West End Press, Cambridge). Stories.

Harvest, 1977 (West End Press, Cambridge). Stories.

A collection of writings by **Meridel Le Sueur** is scheduled for publication in late 1977 by Feminist Press, Old Westbury, N.Y. A novel, **The Girl,** is scheduled for publication by West End Press in late 1977.

Publications of West End Press

 Anticipated dates shown in the case of material awaiting publication. Address inquiries to West End Press, Box 697, Cambridge, Ma. 02139.

Dona Stein, **Children of the Mafiosi** (poems), 1977.
Peter Oresick, **Story of Glass** (poems), 1977; second
    edition, 1977.
Antar Mberi, **Bandages and Bullets** (poems), 1977.
Meridel Le Sueur, **Harvest** (stories), 1977.
    Song for My Time (stories), 1977.
    The Girl (novel), December 1977.
    Worker Writers (teaching text), with Minnesota
        Peoples' History Project, December 1977.
Manny Fried, **Drop Hammer** (play), with Labor Arts
    Books, December 1977.

Subscribe to
West End Magazine

WEST END MAGAZINE is now formally
separate from West End Press, though we still
work together editorially and politically. We
urge you to subscribe to this lively quarterly,
which has published, in the current issue alone,
such writers as Margaret Randall, Hugh Guilder-
son and Batya Weinbaum. Subscription is $5
annually. The back issue of Volume Four is
available in a uniform set for $5.
Send all orders and requests for information
to Gail Kaliss, Editor, WEST END MAGAZINE,
BOX 354, BRONX' NEW YORK 10468.